Praise for *Ghosted and* [...]

"*Ghosted and Breadcrumbed* clearly and expertly guides women out of painful relationships with unavailable men and into the joys of a healthy relationship. If you are in a relationship with a married man or a man who is avoiding a deeper commitment, this is the book for you!"

— **Lonnie Barbach, PhD,** cocreator of the Happy Couple app and coauthor of *Going the Distance*

"*Ghosted and Breadcrumbed* is a must-read for women who unwittingly fall for unavailable men and want to create happy, healthy relationships. Dr. Feuerman draws on her expertise as a marriage and family therapist to provide valuable insights to help women break free of a pattern of dysfunctional relationships once and for all. She's created a practical and compassionate guide, full of case studies and effective strategies to help women better understand themselves, heal, and create the satisfying, loving relationships they deserve."

— **Sharon Martin, MSW, LCSW,** psychotherapist, mental health blogger, and author of *The CBT Workbook for Perfectionism*

"If you've ever wondered why you always seem to have 'a string of bad luck' with men, wonder no more! This book will explain why you've made the choices you have and what you can do to create 'good luck' in love moving forward."

— **Michele Weiner-Davis,** author of *Healing from Infidelity*

"*Ghosted and Breadcrumbed* is as clever and captivating as its title. Any woman who has experienced unrequited love or tried to catch an unavailable or avoidant man will find wisdom here. Marni Feuerman shows the reader how to sort out what is her fault and what is the man's fault and provides techniques derived from cognitive-behavioral therapy, emotion-focused therapy, and mindfulness-based stress reduction to help her move on and be better prepared for love in the future. The book is written primarily for women in heterosexual relationships, but others may find it of value as well."

— **Stan Tatkin, PsyD, MFT,** clinician and founder of the PACT Institute

"Dr. Feuerman digs deep into *why* some women fall for emotionally unavailable men, then gives actionable steps to help them move on and be free to find real intimacy. A must-read for anyone who feels rejected or undesired in a romantic relationship."

— **Julie de Azevedo Hanks, PhD, LCSW,** psychotherapist and author of *The Assertiveness Guide for Women*

GHOSTED

AND

BREADCRUMBED

GHOSTED
AND
BREADCRUMBED

Stop Falling for Unavailable Men
and Get Smart about
Healthy Relationships

Dr. Marni Feuerman

New World Library
Novato, California

New World Library
14 Pamaron Way
Novato, California 94949

The material in this book is intended for education. No expressed or implied guarantee of the effects of the use of the recommendations can be given or liability taken. Names and identifying details of individuals have been changed to protect their privacy.

Text design by Tona Pearce Myers

Library of Congress Cataloging-in-Publication Data

Names: Feuerman, Marni, date, author.
Title: Ghosted & breadcrumbed : stop falling for unavailable men and get
    smart about healthy relationships / Dr. Marni Feuerman.
Other titles: Ghosted and breadcrumbed
Description: Novato, California : New World Library, [2019] | Includes
    bibliographical references and index.
Identifiers: LCCN 2018046748 (print) | LCCN 2018049186 (ebook) | ISBN
    9781608685875 (ebook) | ISBN 9781608685868 (print : alk. paper)
Subjects: LCSH: Man-woman relationships--Psychological aspects. |
    Single women. | Unrequited love.
Classification: LCC HQ801 (ebook) | LCC HQ801 .F478 2019 (print) | DC
    306.7--dc23
LC record available at https://lccn.loc.gov/2018046748

First printing, April 2019
ISBN 978-1-60868-586-8
Ebook ISBN 978-1-60868-587-5
Printed in Canada on 100% postconsumer-waste recycled paper

New World Library is proud to be a Gold Certified Environmentally Responsible Publisher. Publisher certification awarded by Green Press Initiative. www.greenpressinitiative.org

10   9   8   7   6   5   4   3   2   1

This book is lovingly dedicated to my husband, Michael, and our daughters, Jamie and Mandy

»———→

CONTENTS

TRYING TO LOVE SOMEONE UNAVAILABLE

I've written numerous articles on love and relationships for YourTango.com, About.com (which is now DotDash.com), and *Huffington Post*. Of all of these, none has triggered an influx of more personal responses from readers than the one about walking away from an affair with a married man. Read more than 160,000 times in just over a year (and shared over 600 times on social media), this one seems to have struck a nerve.

This book is for any woman who is romantically involved with an emotionally unavailable man — maybe one who is married to someone else. For clarification, I use *emotionally unavailable* to refer to those who put up walls between themselves and other people to avoid emotional intimacy. Attempting to have, or being in, a relationship with someone who is emotionally unavailable can result in feeling rejected,

1

unloved, neglected, and undesired. At times, an emotionally unavailable person's behavior can rise to the level of psychological or emotional abuse. Such relationships are incredibly distressing and often volatile.

While this book is written for women in heterosexual relationships, I know that emotionally unavailable partners can also be an issue for men and in same-sex partnerships. There may be some gender-based differences, but the psychological underpinnings are the same. Therefore, although I address my advice to the female gender throughout this book, the advice is often applicable to anyone in this circumstance.

This book is not intended to shame you. It is intended to help you be self-reflective regarding the parts of yourself you may not like — the parts that are causing your problems. We *all* have parts like these! This book will help you take an inventory of your own behavior and the source of what is misguiding you. It will also teach you how to change your thinking and your behavior so that you move in a healthy, positive direction.

Thanks to millennials and an online dating culture, some new words have entered the vernacular of dating and relationships. We have names to describe what people experience in the dating world today — I used two in the title of this book. Being "ghosted" is when a person you are dating suddenly disappears. Being "breadcrumbed," as the name implies, is when the person you are dating essentially throws you "breadcrumbs" to keep you hanging on but has little or no intention of maintaining a real relationship with you. Another term, "cushioned," refers to someone keeping you as a "plan B." This person may be a downright cheater, or he may just be keeping multiple potential partners in the loop to avoid regret should one not pan out. And another: getting "stashed" is when your partner keeps you apart from other areas of his life. This person is not ready or willing to admit you exist. You haven't met his friends or family, and if you're with him when he runs into any of them, you barely get introduced, and certainly not as his girlfriend. There are new slang terms coming out all the time for these dating experiences. Despite the funny or light connotations of these terms, the experiences are distressing, embarrassing, and painful...nothing to laugh about.

When someone you have been dating suddenly stops communicating and disappears without warning, it can feel hurtful and disrespectful. The more time you have spent with this person, the worse it feels when he suddenly ceases all communication. Sometimes it is done during a long relationship, which can feel traumatic. Unfortunately, the ghosting trend doesn't seem to be going away. The hookup culture and dating apps, along with the anonymity involved, make it easier for people to behave poorly and get away without consequence. On a more serious level, the lack of empathy for others does not bode well for our society.

Ghosting is easier than rejecting someone face-to-face. The discomfort in such direct communication is so unnerving for some people that they fervently dodge it. Meeting someone online at the get-go may limit the sense of social connectedness, making bad social behavior seem less unconscionable. There might even be a desensitization to such dating behavior as it becomes more and more common.

For someone who has negative dating experiences repeatedly, the sense of rejection can take its toll. It's confusing and makes you uncertain about how you should respond or what you should do. Our reactions come in large part from our perception of a situation, event, or cue. But how do you respond when you don't know precisely what has happened? When you have had multiple negative dating experiences, you will start to question yourself, your judgment, and your worthiness. Even if these perceptions are inaccurate, you will still go to that place within yourself.

Men who fail to effectively communicate while dating or in a relationship do so for various reasons, a topic I take up throughout this book. There are men already committed to someone else, and there are men who are not in other relationships but who still put up barriers to intimacy. I hear daily about women who tolerate such men, hoping they will change. The women continue to suffer while relentlessly trying to "crack the code" and break down the wall.

A woman who falls in love with an emotionally unavailable or married man finds herself wasting years of her life holding on, hoping, and praying that he changes (or leaves his wife). When that never happens, she finds herself having squandered the prime years of her life. Dreams of having children are possibly dashed. Dreams of the house with the white picket fence fade away. If the situation blows up, she may find her reputation a shambles as well. The takeaway message I encourage is not one of alarm but one of extreme caution: perhaps more seriously consider dating emotionally (and physically) available men much earlier in your life.

If what you have read so far resonates with you, you may need to develop a deep understanding of why you get yourself into such circumstances in the first place. Why have you made such poor choices? What keeps you going for so long? Why do you think your "love" will cure the man you're dating? Furthermore, can he make real changes before your life passes you by? You need answers and specific strategies to help you move forward, and I will provide them.

Regarding marriage and infidelity, the word *mistress* has been around for ages. Historically, men have frequently "kept" women. These women were often maintained in a certain life-style, most commonly by wealthier men, so that they could be readily available for sexual pleasure. This was a widespread practice among European royalty and the wealthy. Both *mistress* and another common term, *the other woman*, can stir up negative feelings, so I use *affair partner* whenever possible, because it is the most accurate and respectful term and is gender neutral.

I also use the terms *infidelity* and *unfaithful* in this book. Both of them describe cheating behavior and/or sex outside of marriage, and they involve a person betraying his or her spouse and the marriage vows they took. I do not get into specifics regarding what constitutes infidelity (intercourse, oral sex, cybersex, phone sex, and so on). Suffice it to say that there is a person in the triangle — the spouse — who is betrayed by the intimate involvement of a third party (you). Again, these terms are meant to create clear written communication and comprehension in this book.

Is the man entirely to blame for the predicament you are in with him? It is more important to remember that you can't control his behavior; you can only control yours. Despite this, it is worth taking a look at such men, as well. So, what are the psychological underpinnings of men who are emotionally unavailable? In chapter 2, I profile these men so you will know what "type" you are dealing with. I divide them into multiple general categories, though a given man may fit into more than one. Some examples of these are the Sociopath, the Narcissist, the Player, the Tortured Soul, the Addict, and the Opportunist, and I fully describe them, along with their typical behaviors.

As we journey into this area, I answer several questions that you may have asked yourself: Just what kind of person does hurtful things to others? What kind of person says he loves you but mistreats you? Why would someone string you along like this? What kind of person lingers endlessly among multiple relationships? In chapter 2, I address these questions and more.

Chapter 3 explores specifically what is going on with the married cheater and his wife. Is what he's telling you about her true? You might be shocked if you heard her perspective on him. I have yet to see a distressed couple in my office looking for counseling and find that they both have the exact same assessment of their life together. Most of the time, the viewpoints are vastly different. This doesn't mean that either is wrong or right; it just means that all humans interpret events differently. In your relationship, you hear only one side, and you hear it over and over, and it's his side. His side is not the ultimate truth; it's precisely what the term says: *his* side.

So, once you have decided how to handle your emotionally unavailable partner, it may be time to move on. There are all sorts of ways to "leave your lover." Many songs have been written about it. But what is the best way to leave an unavailable or married man that you are in love with and that you have had a relationship with for a long time? Should you "cold-turkey" it? Ghost him? Should you gradually see him less and less? Or maybe you should just start dating other men and hope you fall in love with someone who is available. These are all possible options; we'll look at which is best.

In chapters 4 and 5, rather than try to pin the blame on the men, we delve into why *you* may have a pattern of involvement with these types. Insights into the "whys" of getting involved with unavailable men most readily derive from your family of origin. They can also come from other life experiences and early romantic relationships. Attachment science provides a lot of information about how our early relationships with primary caregivers (such as our parents) create a blueprint for our behavior in future adult romantic relationships. We'll look at this in detail in chapter 5. Suffice it to say that you need to understand your "wiring" in order to "rewire" yourself.

Throughout the remainder of the book, you will also need to face some harsh truths about yourself. You may be behaving dysfunctionally. *Dysfunctional* in this context means "unhealthy or abnormal in relation to others." You are deviating from the norm. You have your own demons to face. You may be drawn to drama, you may have an underlying mental health problem, you might fear intimacy or commitment, or you may have what is known in the addiction arena as *codependency*. There are numerous reasons you might be content with, or putting up with, such circumstances. Although this book is not about making a moral judgment about you, knowing your core values and having a strong moral compass can help guide you in the right direction.

We will also talk about love throughout the book. It's one of the most powerful emotions in the world. No matter how much logic I impart to you, it will be painfully difficult to ignore or change your feelings of love for the person you may now be involved with. That is why I will help you understand the science of love, neurobiology, and attachment. You must also understand what an unhealthy or toxic love is, and what a safe, secure version of love is.

After exploring how and why you find yourself in unhealthy relationships, you may decide to get out of the one you are in. You may feel firm about doing so, or you may have some degree of ambivalence. These are typical reactions. Perhaps you will find you need to reread the first half of the book several times and even get professional support in order to truly grasp *why* you should get out. In later chapters, we will look at *how* you should get out and ways to move on with your life. If you are currently in between relationships, you will learn how to quickly identify whether a potential relationship or partner is healthy. If it, or he, is unhealthy, you will know what to do for self-preservation in order to move on to someone healthy.

I take a strong stance in this book. I do not entertain the idea of staying in toxic circumstances, nor do I discuss strategies to help you cope with an unavailable partner. This book is for the individual who is contemplating getting out of a relationship or who has already decided to get out but is having trouble doing so. This book is also for the individual who is looking for love but continually finds herself in a repetitive pattern when dating. It's not in your best interest to hold out hope for someone playing games with your heart. You deserve better. You deserve a fulfilled life that includes a loving and responsive partner. Instead of being ghosted or breadcrumbed, you can find a person who is reliable, consistent, and honest and who has an open heart for intimacy.

This book is written for any woman struggling with dating and relationships. The examples and case vignettes in this book are real, though I've changed names and altered some unimportant details to maintain confidentiality. The people and situations described are from client experiences, letters I've received, friends or acquaintances I have spoken with, and stories described in social media and blog posts. Many of them are a composite of painful stories I have heard, and I've even included some of my own. The common thread is that each of the women in these stories is involved with an emotionally unavailable man.

No other available book on this topic is so clearly directed at aiding you in moving on from bad relationships. I purposely do not entertain the option of sticking it out while you hope and pray that your guy will change. I do not believe you should take this gamble with your life. No other book goes as deeply into the psychology of *why* you get into such relationships in the first place, to help you gain the clarity and confidence necessary to move on for good. A clear and concise plan for moving forward makes it possible for you to do so with strength and courage.

This book is intended to help you on your journey to finding real and lasting love. You are unlikely to find it in the arms of a man who plays games with your heart or is married to someone else. I write this book with compassion for you, given your situation. I truthfully know from working with thousands of people as a helping professional, as well as from my own life experience, that you can find yourself in a painful relationship or alone, wishing you had someone special in your life. Sometimes this happens by sheer chance, at times through poor decision-making, and other times through a combination of the two. Regardless, you can develop the insight, strength, and skills to make constructive and healthy changes that will provide you with the happy and bright future you deserve.

My intention for this book is to offer you the combined comforts of a loving mother, supportive best friend, and empathic therapist. Drawing from my years as a practicing therapist specializing in relationships, I can guide you to make healthy choices. I guide people this way every day in my work. I have counseled hundreds of women with various relationship struggles and heartache. I assure them, as I now assure you, that change is worthwhile and possible. I thank you for trusting me to help you.

CHAPTER ONE

UNREQUITED LOVE

The Big Picture

The topic of unrequited love may make for an entertaining movie, but if you are experiencing it yourself, it is anything but entertaining. In fact, it may be one of the most painful experiences you ever have. Unrequited love is love that isn't reciprocated in the same amount (or at all) that you are giving. Finding yourself in this circumstance, whether once or as part of a pattern, is not random. As you will come to realize in the pages of this book, unrequited love results from the impact of early history and experiences, especially with your parents. The good news is that you can unlearn the negative patterns and, instead, learn how to both choose and appreciate an emotionally available partner.

Let's take a look at Samantha's story. For the third Christmas (not to mention Thanksgiving and New Year's) Samantha was by herself. Her married boyfriend was supposed to have left his wife by now. After all, he had asked her to be patient, saying he loved her....It would happen any day now. Samantha thought she suffered alone. Many of her friends had real partners. She felt jealous because, while she had a partner too, she spent these holidays alone.

Samantha was like many women in a relationship with a married or otherwise unavailable man. People would ask her why such an attractive, smart, educated, and hardworking woman didn't have a serious boyfriend. She really seemed to have her life together. And although she always answered, "I haven't met the right one yet," she believed that, one day, she would be introducing the right one — the one she was already seeing — to her inner circle...as soon as he got a divorce. She also believed that she could wait. After all, she was only twenty-five.

Single women in relationships with married, noncommittal, or emotionally unavailable men let many years of their lives go down the drain. The chemistry of lust and fantastic sex can keep them in a state similar to addiction. With a married man, the highs are so high that these women have learned to cope with the lows — the "in-between" times of not being able to see or talk to him and of going solo to parties and events. With the emotionally unavailable man, you find yourself going crazy, in a state of high anxiety, wondering why he has not responded to your call or text.

Like Samantha, you have found that a relationship with a married man ensnares you in a web of lies that keeps this relationship hidden. Your friends and family may have met him under the pretense that he is single. Or perhaps no one even knows he exists. Whatever the case may be, your life is an emotional roller coaster.

Being with an unresponsive man who you know is single

and available is another kind of torture. You tell people you have met a "great guy," and you can't deny the chemistry and intense attraction. Yet your friends all wonder why you also seem miserable. You are likely conflicted because this feeling that you call love makes you insecure and anxious at the same time.

Since you have decided to read this book, maybe you're tired of living in a state of constant ambiguity. Perhaps you are seriously asking yourself if you should cut your losses and move on. Or perhaps you are looking for a sign of hope telling you that you should continue to ride this out. Many women enter into such an arrangement unwittingly. Some women do break up with a man upon learning he's married or emotionally unresponsive and, in doing so, cut off a seemingly drama-filled relationship quickly. However, many others stay in roller-coaster relationships anyway.

When He's Emotionally Unavailable: "Isn't my love enough?" you might ask. I can tell you this circumstance has nothing to do with the amount of love or your ability to love. Lust and infatuation maybe, but not love. Love doesn't hurt like this. Real love is balanced and reciprocal. There is a healthy dependency rather than a codependency. In a healthy dependency, you can each count on the other, and you have each other's back. A man in a mutually loving relationship would not make you feel off balance and as if you are going crazy. He would also be completely honest about his feelings and the status of your relationship.

Let's take a look at Michelle's situation. She got set up on a blind date with Mark by a friend. Not blind exactly, because she knew so much about him before they met. He looked adorable in his social media pictures. Just her type. What's more, he looked great on paper. An Ivy League graduate with a professional job, and Jewish like she was — and now, her friend thought they would be perfect for each other.

When they finally met at a noisy bar, it was as if the heavens parted and there was no one else in the place but them. They talked all night and had so much in common. She was sure she had found "the one." When the date ended, and they went their separate ways, she was excited to hear him say he would contact her and definitely wanted to go out again. Then, when he didn't call or text the next day (or the day after…), she became sad and anxious. She replayed the date in her head, wondering what she had done wrong or if she'd misread Mark.

She finally heard from him on Friday and was now faced with deciding whether she would be "too available" if she agreed to see him on Saturday night as he requested. After polling all her friends, she decided to go out with him, and they had an amazing time again. But then the cycle started over, and again she didn't hear from him for several days. She decided to send him a text, and it went unanswered until the next day. All she got was a "sorry so busy" response. What a letdown. But instead of reading the situation for what it was, Michelle just tried harder and obsessed over him more. She could not comprehend how this could be happening, given all the undeniable chemistry they had.

Fast-forward to a few months later, and the "relationship" Michelle had with Mark — if you want to call it that — was filled with constant ups and downs, highs and lows. He could be very sweet and responsive and, at other times, distant and moody. This left her feeling great at times and, at other times, extremely depressed and anxious. It seemed like she was always worried about the relationship and whether Mark was going to break up with her or had found someone else. Mark called her "needy" when she tried to express her feelings to him. She was so confused at that point. She believed she was in love, but she was miserable and her family was always concerned about her.

Leaving someone you love is one of the most difficult things you can ever do. Michelle got in so deep that it seemed impossible. We can see from her story that she completely missed some major red flags. Even she did not know how she turned into the person she did with Mark. She always saw herself as strong and independent, successful at work, and as someone with plenty of friends.

But the essential point is that men like Mark are not capable of loving women back. Their behavior may run the range from manipulative or insensitive to downright emotionally abusive. It's imperative to understand why this happens and how to find a man who will love you back unequivocally. It is also critical to know when and how to get out of this situation before it creates more distress and psychological damage.

When He's Noncommittal: Don't some men get over their fear of commitment? The short answer is, yes, some men do get over their relationship anxiety (a.k.a. "commitment phobia"). If they are going to, though, it will likely happen in a reasonable amount of time! You will also be getting positive signs during the course of your relationship that it is progressing in that direction. You will not see the same anxiety in other areas of this person's life. Truly noncommittal men are just that: incapable of committing. The issues may be too deep-rooted, or the dysfunction too significant, for him to get past his fear. You may notice it in other areas of his life as well, not just in his relationship history.

This is the situation Emily found herself in. She liked so many things about Jake. They had a lot in common, enjoyed each other's company, and had good sexual chemistry. She was in her late twenties and had established herself in a career. She was ready for marriage and thought Jake would make a good husband and father. After a year of dating, he still never brought up their future and certainly not marriage. Every time she wanted to talk about it, he would derail the conversation by picking an ugly fight. He would say that he was not ready, but he could not provide a clear answer about when he might be. Or he would blame it on his uncertain career path.

Emily noticed he had trouble staying at one company and bounced around a lot. She also knew that his parents had had a contentious divorce and a drawn-out custody battle. She did everything she could to reassure him, yet nothing seemed to calm his fear of committing. Emily began to feel tormented by her love for him and her desire for marriage and children.

Men with relationship anxiety can, indeed, be in love with you. However, they have much more difficulty staying in the relationship long term. They also have trouble talking about a future with you. If push comes to shove, they will likely bolt from the relationship. The expectation of commitment makes them fearful. They may struggle with the conflict of dependency versus freedom. Being in love with someone who can't commit to you can become a nightmare.

When He's Already Committed (or Married): Men in this category are emotionally and often physically unavailable. In fact, they already have a girlfriend or have taken vows with someone. Yet you might find yourself involved with or very attracted to one. Don't some men leave their wives for their lovers? The ones who do are usually the ones who have already made a certain plan to leave even before meeting someone new. If this has not happened in your case, then the odds are woefully not in your favor. Instead, there is an extremely slim chance this man will actually leave his wife. And if he does, the probability that things will work out between the two of you are slimmer still. It is nearly impossible to track real statistical data on this subject, but based on what I've gleaned from the research, I'd say that the percentage of relationships of this sort that successfully work out is 10 percent or less. That means there's a 90 percent chance it will not. Would you bet on a horse with a 90 percent chance of losing? Would you get on a plane with a 90 percent chance of crashing? Of course not. Yet if you've chosen a man in the category that I'm discussing here, you've bet your heart and future on the same horrible odds. You might be thinking that you are going to be the exception, that even with such dismal odds, it will work out for you. I can tell you right now: *you are not the exception to the rule.*

Take Beth's situation. She spent years with Jon. In her mind, he was her soul mate. He had virtually every quality she was looking for. The only problem was that he was married. But he had a "special circumstance." He and his wife had a "marriage of convenience." They never had sex, and the marriage was more of a friendship. They both turned a blind eye where cheating was concerned. They were staying together until their youngest daughter went off to college, so she'd have a stable home environment. Beth could see the light at the end of the tunnel: just two more years, and Jon would get a divorce and marry her. This is what Jon *told* her. She had no evidence to the contrary. Plus, she believed he was sincere. This chemistry could not be faked!

Fast-forward two years (by which time Beth was in her midforties). Jon's youngest finally went off to college. Beth knew that any day now Jon would file for divorce, and they could get married and move on with their lives — together. And, true to his word, Jon did get divorced. But then the unthinkable happened: he also broke up with Beth!

While we can only speculate about Jon's real thoughts, it seems that Beth was his "transitional object." She filled a need for Jon and allowed him to tolerate his marriage. So, yes, he was unhappily married, but this didn't necessarily mean he thought seriously about Beth as she did about him. He had essentially used her. Furthermore, about a year after his divorce, he did get married...to someone else!

With many more women in the workplace these days, bonds and friendships more readily develop between women and men. Many of these relationships are with men who are married. Some of these relationships shift from platonic to emotional and then, most frequently, turn physical. Furthermore, women are far more financially independent now and do not need men to secure their futures. We've even reached the point that a woman can have a career and a child entirely without a man. Overall, women have gotten a much bigger part of the pie. Women hold positions of power, run companies, and are millionaires.

Despite so many changes, however, remember that women tend to be more relational and emotional by nature. Men tend to be more logical (problem solvers) and physical. Another issue is that men tend to desire sex more than women do; women's sex drives seem to wane a few years into marriage and more so after kids. Our bodies go through extreme physical changes, while men do not have such significant changes, and their sex drives don't diminish nearly as quickly. However, the shifts in physical intimacy within the marital relationship resulting from these changes in women affect men significantly and may contribute to some men's complex proclivity to stray. A lot less sex than they had early in the marriage isn't what they "signed up for." Being involved with a married man when you are seeking a committed or monogamous relationship can also wreak havoc on your life. Those in such circumstances some-times even describe it as torturous!

When He's Not That into You: This may seem like an "emo-tionally unavailable man" situation, but it can be tricky. The way to think about it may be that this is less about who he is at the core and more about situational unavailability. He will not be available to you, because he just doesn't have those deeper feelings. He may be a very good, high-quality man, but mutual feeling and attraction are a must for any relationship to get off the ground, let alone be sustainable.

Don't personalize the man that just isn't into you. You have choices, too, and I am sure you can remember times when someone liked you and you did not like him back. The craziness comes when you don't (or he doesn't) accept this and move on. In the best-case scenario, the man will be hon-est and direct from the beginning. If this doesn't happen, be intelligent about his behavioral cues. If he doesn't call, text, or pursue you in some way...he's not that into you!

Your situation may involve complicating factors — perhaps he's your boss, your best friend's spouse, or a neighbor. That is, you may find that seeing him is unavoidable. If you do not see him in your regular day-to-day life, consider this an ad-vantage, since all these complicating circumstances just make things more challenging. However, you can successfully with-draw from this relationship, and chapter 7 discusses how.

You will be able to get through a breakup only if you learn to tolerate the pain of the breakup and the pain of being alone. This is the place where so many people habitually fail. The pain becomes unbearable, and so they keep going back. It's not like a regular breakup, when you're no longer in love, or you're dumped, and the door closes completely. If the door is left open, you may walk back through it and return to him. In that case, your situation is similar to that of an alcoholic who can always access alcohol: you both have to find ways to live while knowing that the thing you crave is out there and potentially obtainable.

Again, the painful feelings are entirely normal. You will experience a loss and will have to go through the grief process. Feeling angry, sad, rejected, lonely, and hurt come with the territory. Chapter 9 will help you devise a plan for riding out these difficult emotions. Using the most effective strategies drawn from my years of doing psychotherapy, I offer practical techniques to help you cope with these feelings and get on the path to feeling good again. Loss can put people in a crisis state, and a breakup (with a married man or in the context of another romantic relationship) certainly fits this category. This book will introduce you to coping strategies that help you adjust to the "new normal" that comes when a loss is accepted, and it will guide you as you move forward.

These therapeutic coping strategies, which are thoroughly explained in chapter 9, make up the acronym GET SMART:

- G — Goal orientation
- E — Emotion management
- T — Thought restructuring
- S — Self-soothing
- M — Mindfulness
- A — Attachment style
- R — Reaching out to others
- T — Transformed behavior

Chapter 10 discusses moving on with your life. This will be a natural progression once you have gained some mastery of the strategies for breaking up and tolerating the associated pain, discussed in chapters 7, 8, and 9. If you have moved on from the pain of this loss, most of the battle is done. But, as with anything you are trying to change, maintaining the changes takes energy and effort. The goal will change from getting out of these relationships to figuring out what you want in life (including any future relationship). Chances are you still desire love and partnering up with someone. If so, that's wonderful! But you need to know how to make your life as fulfilling as possible until this happens. When working to move on, there are several vital concepts to keep in mind regarding goal-setting and overall recovery, which we will explore.

We will return to relationship matters in chapter 11, which discusses in depth what a healthy relationship looks like. Information there presents a picture of what *most* people desire in a partner (for example, honesty, responsibility, caring), which will help you reflect on what attributes you find necessary in a romantic relationship (along with deal breakers).

In that chapter, I also spend a lot of time on what makes a relationship healthy. I focus predominantly on emotional and physical accessibility, along with emotional responsiveness and emotional engagement. I also revisit attachment-related concepts and discuss tuning in to your gut feelings and rational thoughts when interacting with potential romantic interests. I will help you develop a successful dating strategy that enables you to recognize red flags and cut off a poor prospect before you get too involved.

Chapter 12 explores how you can figure out whether you could use some professional help in breaking off a relationship, staying broken up, or making better choices when it comes to romance. Some women "relapse" numerous times back into the arms of their lover. They may find it next to impossible to break free, even as their prime years pass by. A self-help book may be all it takes for some, but for many the guidance of a professional counselor provides the support, and facilitates the intensive emotional work, necessary to move forward. The chapter also explains how to find the right professional.

Finally, chapter 13 reviews key points and leaves you with messages about self-love, finding a sense of purpose, and healing. We also look at vulnerability, loss, and forgiveness. You can explore the recommended reading and additional resources that follow the final chapter to help yourself stay on track.

CHAPTER TWO

MAYBE IT'S HIM

Mr. Unavailable Profiled

It's hard *not* to analyze why someone would be averse to intimacy and closeness with others. We have a lot of information from the social science field that says humans are hardwired to connect with others. This phenomenon is part of our evolution and critical to our survival as a species. Yet reality tells us that some seem to choose social isolation. Some people may also refuse to risk the potential rejection that comes when seeking connection with others. These individuals are not going to make themselves vulnerable to that type of emotional risk. Now that we've discussed the big picture in chapter 1, let's take a closer look at science to uncover the deeper reasons why some people avoid connection.

Attachment

It is beneficial to understand the basics of what is called *attachment theory* in the context of dating and relationships. Attachment theory is based upon work by psychologist and researcher John Bowlby that he started in the early 1950s. Attachment is about how we develop deep bonds with those we depend on. The first bond is most often with a parent, since we are not born with the ability to take care of ourselves. We are entirely dependent upon a parent or a substitute caretaker. How reliable and consistent the care is influences our sense of security with ourselves, the world, and others. These early patterns also create a blueprint for how we behave in romantic relationships. The core of this involves how we think about and know what we need and the ways in which we get those needs met. Several patterns, or "styles," evolve from the safety and security of this initial relationship. We have either *a secure attachment style* or one of three possible *insecure attachment styles*.

A person with a secure attachment style is able to easily identify his or her needs and be comfortable reaching for other people to get those needs met if necessary. Securely attached people are also at ease meeting the needs of others, such as a romantic partner. In general, this style emerges from an overall happy childhood with consistent caregivers who met both the physical and the emotional needs of the child. The three insecure styles are anxious, avoidant, and disorganized.

Those who have an *anxious attachment style*, also known as "ambivalent" or "preoccupied," seek a lot of reassurance, as these names imply, and become anxious when separated from a partner. Sometimes, they are viewed as "too needy" or simply "insecure." This is often the result of inconsistent caregiving in childhood or a highly anxious parent.

Those with an *avoidant attachment style*, also known as

"dismissive," minimize their need for others or even deny having such needs. This frequently arises from the unavailability of a caregiver early in life, which left the child to take care of him- or herself or manage difficult emotions alone. Their view of relationships is quite negative.

The last category, *disorganized attachment style*, is also known as *fearful-avoidant*. People with this style often desire intimacy and connection but fear them at the same time. Hence, they give a lot of mixed signals and display "come here / go away" behavior. This style is often a result of childhood abuse, trauma, or severe inconsistency in parenting.

Typical behaviors of those who have any of the insecure attachment styles can also be viewed as coping strategies. They may have worked well in childhood or perhaps were needed for survival, but they work poorly in adult romantic relationships. For instance, a person who avoids conflict at all costs may be reacting to early bad memories of conflict within the family.

It's important to know that we all have an attachment style. Attachment styles should not be considered normal versus abnormal. Your attachment style is affected by not just the quality of your parenting but the quality of your experiences with others throughout your life. It is significantly affected by how secure you feel (or don't feel) within a relationship and how you respond to feelings of disconnection. Attachment is also a topic separate from mental illness. Some people may have a mental illness, "bad genetics," a personality disorder, immaturity, or some combination of these things that is to blame for their transgressions or uncaring behavior.

Types of Emotionally Unavailable Men

Who are these men who behave poorly in romantic relationships? Do they all have an insecure attachment style? I would venture to say that many of them do. I have categorized these men using "profiles" that characterize their typical behaviors both when dating and when relating.

The Married (or Already in a Serious Relationship)

The ultimate unavailable man is the one who is already committed in some capacity to someone else. This person will also fit some of the other profiles listed below. I thoroughly explore this situation in chapter 3.

The Long-Distance Lover

You and he do not live in the same area. Such relationships often become passionate, and when you do see each other it is exciting and fantasy-like. I am definitely not saying that these relationships never work out. I know that they can, and not all participants in this type of relationship are emotionally unavailable. But some are, and purposely do not seek relationships with those they can see regularly. Just beware of how easy it is for him to hide from you who he really is. In fact, some men may purposely choose someone who won't be privy to their day-to-day life for any number of reasons. Keep in mind that you *must* live in the same area to actually get to know each other and see if your relationship can really work out.

The Personality-Disordered

Perhaps he is a narcissist or, worse, a sociopath. Regardless, he keeps you around for his own exploitive or opportunistic purposes. He may be looking for validation of his good looks, virility, and manliness. He may lack both empathy and sensitivity to how his actions affect you. His feelings are the only ones that really matter. He is likely charming and confident as well, which can quickly suck you in.

This type might just be using you. He could be getting what he can for his own good out of being with you. This is not always sex. You may be offering him a place to stay or financially supporting him. If he is married, you may be the transitional person to help him out of his marriage. Regardless, love is not his motive.

Those with personality disorder traits also have the uncanny ability to make you feel like you are the one with the problem. He may be capable of committing to you in some respects, but understand that he will never love you as much as he loves himself. He may be in a position of high power owing to his career, wealth, political position, fame, or all of the above, and women often find this extremely attractive. Those in positions of leadership, control, and power are often admired by others and effortlessly capture the romantic attention of women. Just remember: he expects to be the "dotee" not the "doter."

The Nonmonogamous

This man is incapable of monogamy or will pretend to value faithfulness but be unable to sustain it. He may lie to keep you as a sexual partner for as long as possible. He may have a sex addiction, only view women as objects, or think monogamy is boring. This guy may be a player already involved with others, or he might not tell you he's married. You may find out on your own, or he may drop a bombshell after you are heavily involved. He is good at compartmentalizing and keeping secrets. He is also good at hiding his other dates while keeping you in the running. There is a coldness or an aloofness about him. He can keep you off balance, making you feel desired one moment and ignored the next.

The Addict

A man of this type has some chemical involvement (a drug or alcohol problem) that causes him to be inconsistent in his behavior. The behavior may run the gamut from being "out of it" to being aloof to being hyper when you are around. You may not know he has an addiction at all, because many addicts are creative at hiding it. Your gut may tell you that something is wrong, but you can't put your finger on it. If, and when, you find out, everything seems to click. Unless you want to get high with him or be his enabler, you need to run.

A trickier addiction is addiction to work. Workaholism is still a socially acceptable addiction. You may certainly admire him for his fantastic work ethic at first. Before long, though, you will feel the frustration of lonely nights and events missed because of his work schedule or constant meetings. Your guy should be working hard but not working constantly with zero work/life balance. An addict will not be there for you in your times of need, leaving you hurt and disappointed. The only thing you can rely on is his unreliability.

The Hot Mess

This man is emotionally unavailable (perhaps temporarily) owing to some tragedy or misfortune occurring in his life. A hot mess may have just lost his job or someone close to him. He may very well be a great guy, but the timing is unfortunate. Getting involved now is not a good idea. Keep in touch from a distance, and wait for him to get back on his feet before you consider anything more serious.

Another man may be more seriously impaired for the long run. He might be a "mama's boy," or maybe he's too close to his sister or his buddies. He has a weak sense of self and is too needy and dependent on his current attachments to properly engage in a healthy adult relationship. His emotions are tied up in others, leaving little or no room for you. Alternatively, he may have trouble saying no to others. His boundary blurring will suck up all his energy and the time that he could be spending with you. He has to work out these dysfunctional dynamics before he is ready for a mature relationship with you.

The Straight-Up Avoider

A man such as this experiences much ambivalence about relationships and commitment. He is the type who has feelings for you but, because of past bad experiences or a bad childhood, isn't able to commit or show consistency. This is the guy you can never seem to get close to. He holds his cards close to the vest. He doesn't share his feelings and is evasive when asked. He may stonewall you when you fight, shutting down and refusing to talk. It is incredibly frustrating for you to have his physical presence but no emotional presence. The more you push, however gently, the more you are pushed back.

With this type of man, you will never develop the closeness and connection required for a successful long-term relationship. He may epitomize the fearful-avoidant attachment style: he might desire intimacy and closeness but get freaked out by it at the same time. He may be holding resentment because of his last broken heart. He may seem like a "victim" of circumstance. Or he may just be cynical and depressive, unable to get out of his own head. He might also be the one you had a great first date with, but then — poof — he disappears. Life is incredibly complicated for this person. This one may be the most innocent of the bunch, and you might be tempted to continue with him to be helpful or because you feel so sorry for him. It is, however, a terrible idea to do so.

I have tried to make this list of profiles as exhaustive as possible so you can get a sense of the characteristics commonly seen in people who are emotionally unavailable. As you can see, there is a variety of men who are emotionally unavailable for many different reasons. We have some idea of the reasons these men are the way they are and act the way they do. Much of it is likely explained through the lens of attachment theory. A lot is also explained by the man's personal life experiences and situations, both past and present, that influence him. We can't leave out the genetic or biological influences, either. The good news is that you do not necessarily have to know the exact reason why a man is acting as he is to make the changes you desire in yourself and find a healthy and loving relationship.

Emotional Unavailability Checklists

Here are two checklists of some signs indicating that the man you are with is emotionally unavailable. Take a pencil and put a checkmark next to the ones that apply to your current situation. (If you are not currently dating or in a relationship, think about your last relationship.) If you have checked off several items on this list, it is very likely you are with an emotionally unavailable man.

❑ He has a wife or a girlfriend.
❑ He ruminates about a past relationship or frequently talks about how much an ex hurt him.
❑ He seems detached or cold.
❑ He seems unresponsive to my feelings or needs.

❑ He keeps himself listed on a dating app or website while dating me.

❑ He does not introduce me to friends or family.

❑ He excludes me from important parts of his life.

❑ He keeps exes around and calls them all friends.

❑ He can go for days without contacting me and is difficult to get in touch with.

❑ He won't spend any money on me (but spends it on himself without a problem).

❑ He stresses that he needs a lot of "space" or time to himself.

❑ He seems to constantly get angry at the little things.

❑ He has a lot of difficulty articulating his feelings.

❑ He avoids conflict or quickly shuts down during an argument.

❑ He dismisses me easily.

❑ He rarely asks how I'm doing (or about my day / my thoughts / my feelings).

❑ He lacks self-confidence or gets down on himself easily.

❑ He won't leave anything at my place.

❑ He won't let me leave anything at his place.

❑ He has said he can't stand "needy" women (which many of his exes seem to be).

❑ He says all his ex-girlfriends are crazy.

❑ He avoids affection or physical intimacy (except sex).

❑ He does not update his relationship status on social media.

❑ His mood can change at the drop of a hat.

❑ He avoids talking about deep or difficult topics.

❑ He evades questions about our future.

❑ He refuses any "relationship" talks or discussions about "us as a couple."

- ❑ His view of relationships seems unrealistic or akin to romantic fantasy.
- ❑ He is selfish, self-centered, or self-absorbed.
- ❑ He is hypercritical or seemingly nitpicks at a lot of things.
- ❑ He has said outright that he fears commitment.

Tune in to your gut feelings about the man you are dating or are in a relationship with. If you check off a few of the following statements, then, here again, it is likely you are with someone emotionally unavailable.

I think and feel as if...

- ❑ I don't know whether I am coming or going in this relationship.
- ❑ I don't really know him.
- ❑ I don't know where I stand with him.
- ❑ I am not appreciated.
- ❑ I am not important.
- ❑ I never seem to be on his mind.
- ❑ He brings out the worst in me.
- ❑ I am in a constant state of anxiety.
- ❑ I am manipulated or fooled by him.
- ❑ My self-esteem is plummeting.
- ❑ I am uncharacteristically suspicious or jealous.
- ❑ I am preoccupied with him and the relationship.
- ❑ I would get nothing from him if I didn't push for it.
- ❑ I am the only one bringing up important topics to discuss.
- ❑ I am the only one who discusses our future together.
- ❑ I can be abandoned by him at any minute.
- ❑ I am last on his list of priorities.
- ❑ I must up the ante to get his attention.
- ❑ My gut is trying to tell me to move on.

Sometimes, the signs are subtle. Let's take a look at the example of Amanda and Sam. They were set up by friends. When they met, they hit it off right away. They had a lot in common, and there was a strong physical attraction. Their relationship followed an ordinary course in the beginning. Sam was consistent and always called when he said he would. There truly was no way to know that Sam was emotionally unavailable until several months into the relationship.

It wasn't a dramatic shift but a gradual one accompanied by a handful of red flags. For instance, after their first fight, Amanda was upset but thought she and Sam should discuss everything and try to resolve things. Sam wouldn't talk to Amanda at all. He just refused to address it. Amanda became even more distressed at being shut out. After three days of stone-cold silence, he called her as if nothing had happened. She was perplexed but also relieved that he'd finally reached out, so she didn't bring it up. But then it happened again. Amanda got shut out and was let back in only when Sam was ready.

She also began to sense that Sam would talk about topics only on a superficial level. He never talked about his feelings. He would get evasive and uncomfortable when she would ask. Amanda realized that if she stayed with Sam, she would be doing all the emotional heavy lifting in their relationship. She asked him if he would go to a counselor with her to try to resolve this, because they were getting serious and she loved him. She was heartbroken that he refused and stated, "I am who I am. Do not try to change me." Amanda made the painful but smart decision to break up with him because she knew she wanted to connect deeply with a partner. She also needed someone who would not abandon her after a fight or disagreement. Sam was a "straight-up avoider," and Amanda stayed clearheaded enough to see the signs and tune in to her gut feelings.

On the other end of the spectrum, the signs are much more apparent. Some women find themselves in a particularly hellish existence with a sociopath or a narcissist. These men go beyond emotional unavailability by also being emotionally abusive. Take Laura and Craig. Laura was kindhearted and caring but naive. She was swept off her feet by Craig in the beginning. A few months into their relationship, he began to get jealous and controlling. She constantly had to reassure him of her love and commitment. Sometimes, he would fly off the handle at her over small things.

She began to question her sanity and would blame herself for upsetting him. He would go from loving to ice cold at the drop of a hat. When she tried to break up with him, he would cry and say he would change, but it never lasted long. She really wanted to end the relationship but worried about hurting him and ended up feeling trapped. It took a friend, her family, and a therapist to help her find the strength to finally get out.

Emotional Unavailability versus Emotional Abuse

I'd like to be clear about what constitutes *emotional unavailability* and what constitutes *emotional abuse*. It can be a very fine line. Abuse is not always as obvious as being hit or shoved, called degrading names, or cussed out. In fact, it can very well be underhanded or subtle. You may find yourself feeling confused about the relationship, off balance, or as if you are walking on eggshells all the time. This is the kind of abuse (also called mental abuse or psychological abuse) that can sneak up on you as you become more entrenched in the relationship.

Psychological abuse occurs when one person in the relationship tries to control information available to the other person to manipulate his or her viewpoint or sense of reality. This abuse often contains strong, emotionally manipulative themes and threats intended to make the victim acquiesce. In addition, most abusive partners are skilled at convincing the victim that the abuse is his or her fault. Somehow, the victim is responsible for what happened. If the abuse causes you to doubt your own memory, perception, or sanity, this means you are being "gaslighted." Examples may range from the abuser denying that previous abusive incidents ever occurred to staging bizarre events with the intention of confusing you.

Abusers at times will throw you a bone, so to speak. I have heard too many times that a partner was "nice," "complimentary," "gave me a gift," and so on, as if this should erase all the bad treatment. You need to understand that this is part of the dynamic and cycle of abuse. In fact, it is rare for abusive relationships to not have these (often intense) moments of feeling good, excessively sincere apologies, or attempts to make up for the bad behavior. These moments can cause you to cling to the hope that the relationship will change, and the abuser knows this.

It's important to remember that emotional abuse is absolutely not your fault. Abusers are expert manipulators with a knack for getting you to believe that the way you are being treated is your fault. These people know that everyone has insecurities, and they use your insecurities against you. Abusers are adept at convincing you that you do not deserve better treatment, or that they are treating you this way to "help" you. Some abusers even act charming in public so that others have a good impression of them. In private it's a different story, which is baffling. Given that this abuse is cunning and hard to recognize, I have included a checklist that will help you more easily tell when it is occurring.

Emotional Abuse Checklist

If the man you are seeing displays even a handful of the following signs, you are in an emotionally abusive relationship.

- ❏ He humiliates or embarrasses you.
- ❏ He supplies constant put-downs.
- ❏ He is hypercritical.
- ❏ He refuses to communicate.
- ❏ He ignores or excludes you.
- ❏ He has extramarital affairs.
- ❏ He engages in provocative behavior with the opposite sex.
- ❏ He frequently uses sarcasm and an unpleasant tone of voice.
- ❏ He displays unreasonable jealousy.
- ❏ He exhibits extreme moodiness.
- ❏ He makes mean jokes or constantly makes fun of you.
- ❏ He says "I love you but...."
- ❏ He says things like "If you don't _____, I will _____."
- ❏ He exhibits domination and control.
- ❏ He withdraws affection.
- ❏ He guilt-trips you.
- ❏ He makes everything your fault.
- ❏ He isolates you from friends and family.
- ❏ He uses money to control you.
- ❏ He constantly calls or texts you when you are not with him.
- ❏ He threatens to commit suicide if you leave.

If you now realize that you are in a relationship with someone abusive, I urge you to get out — with professional help if needed. You may feel that you love this person, but he does not love you or respect you. I assure you that, in time, you will get over this person if you break it off. You are worthy of a kind, loving, and respectful relationship.

If you recognize yourself in these descriptions and stories and are finding that you must face the reality of your situation — your entanglement with someone emotionally unavailable (or, worse, emotionally abusive) — you are in a decidedly tough spot. No one wants to let go when the feelings of lust or good chemistry have already taken hold. The following chapters will guide you to fully understand why and how you may have ended up in this situation now or repeatedly. They will also provide you with a road map to letting go and explain why doing so is vital.

CHAPTER THREE

BEING THE AFFAIR PARTNER

A Dead-End Street

This chapter is dedicated to the woman who has found herself in love with the quintessentially unavailable partner — the one already married. The affair may be an emotional affair or both a physical and an emotional one. An emotional affair is a relationship with someone married that is close and intimate but without physical contact. These often morph into full-blown physical affairs because usually there is undeniable chemistry between the two individuals. Quite often, a woman drawn into such a relationship had no intention of having an affair with someone married. If you have had such an affair, you might say that "it just happened." Another scenario is that you did not even know he was married when you met. He put himself out there as single. When you found out, perhaps you had already fallen in love. Regardless of how this relationship came to be, such situations are particularly distressing when you want more — when you want him all to yourself.

It repeatedly happens that women enmeshed in affairs become anguished while deciding what to do with this kind of relationship. Most likely they fit the description of one of the three types of insecure attachment styles. Furthermore, certain personality traits considered virtuous and positive may create a double-edged sword for these women — for example, being empathic, hopeful, strong-willed, passionate, and loving. These women have a natural tendency to empathize with a man's situation if he is unhappily married. A strong-willed nature and hopefulness keep them holding out for a happy ending. These are passionate women, and they finally have someone who appreciates it. Having a loving nature makes it a challenge to merely stop loving him and think that there might be someone else to love! If you are in this predicament, your good intentions have serious unintended consequences.

Take Kathy's situation. She considers herself an "empath," someone who easily becomes attuned to other people's energy. Empaths intuitively perceive and experience the feelings of others. The danger for empaths comes when they also take on the emotions of others. They may even do so at the expense of their own needs. Women like Kathy frequently attract their opposite — those deficient in empathy, such as sociopaths and narcissists.

Kathy felt Matthew's pain very deeply. He always looked distressed, and when she asked him if everything was okay, he took the opportunity to pour his heart out about his troubled marriage and how his wife didn't appreciate him despite the many things he did to try to please her. Kathy felt a pull to comfort him, and of course, she felt so bad about his circumstances. He seemed like a great guy. Before long, she was doing way too much to comfort Matthew. The boundaries between his own pain and her pain for him became utterly blurred. She was in a full-fledged affair by the time she realized she had made a huge mistake. Interestingly enough, now *she* could never do enough to please Matthew. In his eyes, she was always doing something wrong. Then, it dawned on her that she was probably feeling the way his wife felt — Matthew never believed he got enough care, love, and attention; he was always unsatisfied.

Women pursue relationships with men who are already taken based on their feelings and chemistry. The men, however, may only be looking to fill a need. Some men act out of selfishness and self-righteousness — they just want the physicality of the relationship with you. But those trying to fill an unmet emotional need aren't simply focused on the physical. If they've been rejected by their wives, they may also feel unloved, unimportant, or hurt. Hence, the problem-solving state of mind: "I can stay happily married (or at least somewhat satisfied) and keep my family intact by maintaining an affair." This probably isn't a conscious thought, but it is likely a factor at play.

The profiles of unavailable men discussed in chapter 2 are also typical of married men who have affairs. However, if you have fallen for a married man, he most likely fits the narcissist profile. It is easy to get fooled by this type of person. Narcissistic people are often especially attractive and charismatic. They appear self-assured and confident. Others perceive them positively even before having any sort of interaction (a phenomenon called *zero acquaintance*)! Ironically, though, others' perceptions become highly unfavorable as time goes on.

Married men who have affairs tend to have been avoidant in their past relationships, and they surely are with their current spouse. They don't face problems head-on. They lack proactive behavior and problem-solving skills. They avoid confrontation. They turn to someone outside their marriage to get their needs met or as a coping strategy of sorts. They often come from dysfunctional families. They may have had cheating parents, or they saw a cold and unloving relationship between their parents.

The chances are excellent that the married man you are involved with picked you opportunistically. He may have some feelings for you, but it's more probable that he just enjoys the physical aspect and excitement of the relationship. He is absorbed in the fantasy and fun that this relationship brings. And if he actually did leave his wife for you, you both would eventually find yourselves in a regular relationship. Following the stereotype, he would tire of your nagging, overspending, or PMS-ing, and you would tire of his clothes on the floor, his spontaneous farting, and his tuning you out every Sunday for football. And if in fact he is a narcissist, you are heavily involved with someone insensitive, self-absorbed, and manipulative.

Magical Thinking

Men who are cheating on their wives are not the "good ones." These are not men of integrity. You can easily get caught up in magical thinking about the relationship you have with this type of man. Magical thinking may also come up for you when you consider someone not necessarily taken but emotionally unavailable. Here are some examples of this thinking:

- He really loves me; he made a mistake getting married to her.
- He would never cheat on me once we're together for real.

- His wife must really be so _____ (fill in the blank: bitchy, cold, nasty...).
- He's my soul mate; there can't possibly be anyone else out there for me.
- We have a special connection.
- I am supposed to be understanding because _____ (fill in the blank: he has a child, he is a victim of a bad circumstance...).
- I can make him happy in a way she couldn't.

You get the point. This thinking will keep you in this ongoing cycle of highs and lows with this person.

Common Threads among Affair Partners

Affair partners tend to experience one or more of several themes. Here are some of them:

- It is often a lonely and isolating experience. You might have to keep this part of your life hidden from friends and family. You often suffer in silence.
- You have one of the three insecure attachment styles that gets activated by your married partner.
- You may not have known your partner was married when you met, and now that you have fallen in love you're already thinking it's too late to get out.
- You experience a great deal of anxiety (fear, rumination) because you are involved with someone married.
- You recognize that your values do not align with your actions.
- You try to focus much more on the positives of the relationship and reasons to stay the course.
- You invest a lot of time, resources, and energy in the relationship, making it hard not to see it through.

What's the Deal with His Wife?

You are probably very curious about your man's wife. You view her as a rival who is standing in the way of your happiness. You may know her personally, or she may be a stranger. Regardless, your perception and knowledge of her are based mostly on what your man tells you (and doesn't tell you). If your man does talk about her, you probably hear all the horrible things she does. If you know her and see her in a good light from your experience, you may not know what to think. His words don't fit what you see or know. However, if you don't know her, you can easily believe his convincing point of view. In fact, you will do whatever you can *not* to be like her. You will want to prove to him that you can make him happy. It's part of the cycle that keeps you hooked.

Some men won't even mention their wives. They refuse to discuss her or become quite good at evading any questions about her or the marriage. They have superior compartmentalization skills. This will drive you nuts! You will do whatever you can to try to find out about her. You will also look for reasons to consider her awful, to justify your behavior with her spouse.

Diana did just that. She was Jon's affair partner for several months. He would not tell her why he was unhappy with his marriage. She stalked his wife on Facebook and saw that she and his wife had a friend in common. First, she was taken aback by how pretty his wife was. Diana made up a silly reason to ask her friend about Jon's wife. She was even more disheartened to hear that the friend thought so highly of her, saying she was thoughtful and kind.

There are several primary reasons (excuses?) your man will give you to explain why he is having an affair. I list some of them here so you can recognize that hearing them may keep you stuck trying to be the one to make this relationship work.

- "I'm not in love with her anymore." He may not understand how love evolves over the course of a long-term relationship. He is also equating love with lust.
- "She never wants to have sex" or "The sex is boring." For many, the novelty and excitement of married sex will never compare to the excitement of affair sex. The spouse may be very attractive and sexy too…it really doesn't matter.
- "She doesn't take care of herself" or "She gained a lot of weight." Your man will highlight her undesirable traits and how she has let herself go.
- "She doesn't understand me." This is a big cliché and probably a big lie. The wife knows him all too well, and this bothers him.
- "She's a nag." This may be true in some regard. But, as a couples' therapist, I can tell you that the more one partner withdraws and avoids, the more the spouse nags, pokes, and pushes for intimacy, connection, and closeness.
- "She doesn't appreciate me." This one often has some truth to it as well. It does not excuse the cheating behavior, however. Cheating is not a solution to the marital problem.
- "She is mentally ill." It is possible his wife is physically or mentally ill (or both). Your man may worry about how his wife will decompensate if he leaves. He may also worry about a severe reaction or breakdown.

If he tells you they are both unhappy but won't divorce, you may hear these reasons:

- "I can't afford to get a divorce." Facing significant financial changes can definitely be a barrier to seeking a divorce. Many husbands worry about how they will support two separate households or pay alimony. Wives also worry about how they will live off drastically reduced incomes. There may be other money-related intricacies as well. Finances can keep two unhappily married people together.
- "My wife is ill." A man usually will not leave a wife with a chronic medical illness or a wife who is fragile. He may also stay if she is at risk of suicide or deep depression.
- "I will never see my kids." He may fear that his wife will alienate him from the kids or that he will not get fair visitation rights. He may even have discussed this with a lawyer and have good reason to be scared. Or he may tell you, "I will scar my kids." He is afraid of the harm and upheaval it will cause for his children. He wants an intact household and believes it is best for the children if he does not divorce.
- "Leaving my wife for you will negatively affect my career / my reputation / what friends and family think of me / what clients or customers think of me."

Courting Disaster

When involved with a married man, you are courting disaster. This disaster will likely be one of three things: (1) he'll dump you; (2) his wife will find out, and he'll drop you; or (3) he'll leave his wife for you, and together you'll crash and burn. Let's take a look at each of these three scenarios.

Why would this man dump you? Remember, even traditional relationships end for various reasons. He might dump you if he feels too pressured to commit to you or spend time with you. He might dump you because his guilty conscience gets the best of him. He might dump you because he basically doesn't love you anymore. Let's say your man's wife finds out. Or, she kinda, sorta, knew something was up but didn't act on that intuition until now. What if she goes ballistic and seeks revenge on you?

Marcy found out her husband, Dan, the CEO of a highly respected nonprofit organization, was cheating on her with an employee. She stormed into his office one day and literally destroyed it in a rage. He was fired on the spot along with the woman at work he was cheating with. The incident blew them both out of their fantasy world in an instant. He had to search for jobs all across the country because his reputation was destroyed. He couldn't afford the nice family home anymore and moved into a small apartment with a roommate. What had happened created fodder for gossip for a long time after. This may seem like an extreme example, yet it does happen, and it can easily happen to you.

If your man's wife finds out, he will be faced with making a decision whether to stay or go. The energy that goes into this decision is immense. He may very well have feelings for both you and his wife. But he made a commitment to his wife, and if he has children with her, he is very likely going to lean into the marriage, not out of it. Regardless, this will create a severe crisis and much turmoil for him. He may even go into marriage therapy with his spouse at this point. In fact, he may want you to "wait in the wings" while he tries this out. I have seen men come to therapy with their wives, blown away by how devastated their wives are over the affair. The men didn't know how much their wives loved them before this. Often, they both realize that they took each other for granted.

Steve had been married to Kate for fifteen years. They had two kids. He wasn't unhappy with Kate, but in his mind, she seemed to constantly want romance and intimacy. She always wanted to talk, to improve their communication. As a relatively withdrawn guy, Steve didn't like to talk about their problems. If he was angry at Kate, he thought it would be better to just ignore it and let things settle down.

Steve met Jodi at work. He found her easy to have a relationship with. She never brought up anything serious and was a lot of fun. Steve, being unable to maturely communicate with his wife, had this affair to get some relief from the seriousness of day-to-day family life. Kate did find out about the affair and was devastated. All she'd done was try to love Steve. She had no idea why he would do this to her.

The story you get from your man, or what you piece together with limited information, is not the entire truth. Most importantly, you deserve someone fully available to be your partner. You also deserve honesty and transparency and should not settle for less than that, ever.

Several chapters of this book explore the reasons women stay with unavailable men. However, regarding the man who is married, we also need to examine some additional special circumstances that may keep you hooked. The foremost special circumstance is the promise of commitment or marriage or that he will leave his wife for you down the road. Your viewpoint on this notion may vary. In his eyes, your relationship might be a long-term ongoing secret affair. In your eyes, it is a love affair, and there is hope that commitment will come. He may even offer a time frame. You will likely see this time frame get pushed back over and over. You might hear a lot of reasons why it can't happen soon. Meanwhile, you wait and wait and wait. If you desire children, you might be forced to give up on this, too, while waiting. Again, you deserve a fulfilling life. Your goals must be front and center and supported by a life partner instead of compromised by him.

Let's say that, as a result of failed marriage therapy, a mid-life crisis, or his own personal decision, he does leave his wife for you. Unfortunately, your relationship with him is probably doomed to fail. It may seem cynical of me to say this, but I assure you, this is the honest, direct, and realistic assessment of what will most likely occur. As noted earlier, only the tiniest of chances exists for the relationship to succeed if it began as an affair — a possibility so slim that I can't in good conscience advise you to bet on it.

This relationship is doomed to fail for several reasons:

Reason #1: The relationship got off to a troubling start. It was based on deceit and dishonesty. Does that sound like a good beginning to you? I am not sure if any woman (or man) looking for love would ever say, "I would like a dishonest person."

Reason #2: You have been living in a fantasy world. You got his best side. You two have always done something fun, romantic, or sexual. There has likely also been much novelty, which added to the rush of endorphins you got whenever you saw him. You did not get to see everything about him, and therefore you have built up a certain false image of him.

Reason #3: You will now be involved in his day-to-day life. If he's in a crisis over choosing you over his marriage, he will not be as present, fun, or exciting. He may even start to have difficulty sexually. You will get to see all his habits, quirks, and moods. You may decide you don't like them. You may decide you don't like *him*.

Reason #4: He may realize you are not right for him now that he is with you full-time. If he's like many cheating men, you served a purpose while he was married, but now you are no longer needed. Or, he (or you) will decide you both are not a match now that you are in a regular relationship.

Reason #5: His extended family, children, and friends will dislike you. You will be seen as a home-wrecker or worse. You may not be welcomed by his family and friends. If he gets serious about choosing to marry or live with you, are you ready to be a stepmother? How well do you think this transition is going to go over with the children? Having stepchildren puts significant stress on even the healthiest remarriages.

Reason #6: Good men do not cheat. They work on the problems in their marriages. He will not magically morph into a good guy just because he is now with you. His behavior — call it immoral, narcissistic, egotistical, or just plain being a jerk — is part of *him*, whether he's married, divorced, or single.

Reason #7: Will you ever really trust him? Now that you've got the guy, do you feel deep down that he would not choose to have another affair, with someone else? You might not be able to let your guard down and relax even though he is with you now.

Reason #8: You will be forever branded as the "other woman." Anyone who has met you or knows you by way of these circumstances will never view you differently. It may seem unfair, but this is powerful stuff and one of those things that can stay with you.

Reason #9: You might feel extreme culpability over what has happened. If he is now an outcast according to his family and friends, you might feel terrible about it. This guilt is actually healthy, because it means you have now realized you were part of creating this problem. You did do something wrong. However, the guilt can seriously eat away at you and cast a dark cloud over your head.

Reason #10: His former wife will still be in your life if they have children. If the discovery of the affair and the resultant divorce was a shock to her, you might become the target of her anger. Inside, she may still feel shock and despair. Her world has crumbled, and she is grieving. This may affect you directly or indirectly if she continues to make her ex-spouse miserable.

You may have begun to recognize that you are entitled to more than an already-taken man. So how do you get yourself out? Perhaps you have tried a few times only to be lured back in. You may have been experiencing a lot of ambivalence about this arrangement. Or you may still be hoping things will end somehow, some way, with your heart intact.

If you have made the decision to do what it takes to get out, I applaud you. To make this happen, you will have to take a good hard look at yourself. You will need to understand the underlying reasons that you got caught up in something like this. The same applies if you are in any other kind of unhealthy relationship, whether it involves emotional unavailability, abuse, addiction, or any type of toxic behavior. You need an in-depth understanding of why you engage in specific unhealthy behaviors or you'll be destined to repeat them, maybe not in exactly the same circumstances, but in similar ones.

CHAPTER FOUR

MAYBE IT'S YOU

Why on earth would someone continue to put herself repeatedly in situations that cause her pain? It is a question that may be unanswerable in its entirety, but we can certainly look at some of the potential reasons. Looking at yourself in the mirror is no easy task. Most of us either avoid it or operate from the perspective that we don't need to do it. Insight levels relating to self-perception can fluctuate widely. People can go from having an immense amount of insight to having nearly none. People vary on a continuum ranging from extremely psychologically healthy to severely disordered. And unquestionably, people vary significantly in their motivation, and perhaps ability, to make personal changes. Given this phenomenon, I ask you to stay open-minded enough to explore and consider what you are about to read in this chapter.

Let's break down the reasons you may repeatedly find yourself falling for men who won't, or can't, love you back. I emphasize again that this is tough to explore. It may bring up some feelings of sadness, anger, or shame. This is normal, however, because it is impossible to scrutinize our flaws without some of these feelings coming up. The good news about having these emotions is that emotion can be a huge motivator. Think about anything you do in life. If you didn't feel emotionally moved to do it, you wouldn't do it! Commonly, the only other time we do what we do is to avoid punishment or some other negative consequence. Strangely, people can suffer many adverse effects in a lousy relationship yet keep forging ahead. When it comes to matters of the heart, our feelings can guide us to what we need to do to feel better. So, let's now take a look at some of the reasons that may be contributing to your relationship choices.

You Are the Intimacy Avoider (Not Him)

You make a habit of avoiding real love as a way of protecting yourself. It's also a way to keep from getting hurt. It seems counterintuitive, since you are getting hurt anyway, but you may just be getting the sensation of being in love without real risk. It is impossible for the relationship to go very deep. You don't have to know your partner on a deeper level, and he doesn't get to know you either. Wanting a relationship and wanting emotional intimacy are two different things.

Chasing and pursuing an impossible person becomes a trade-off of sorts. You satisfy your longing for connection along with your need to protect your vulnerable feelings. Remaining fixated on someone who doesn't show genuine love for you allows you to feel the intensity and passion involved in a relationship without eventual commitment. But worse than that, you are often not seeing the real potential partners that may be right in front of you!

Taylor was the one who avoided intimacy, and she had no idea. After all, she'd been with Hunter for three years already. Taylor owned her own business and did quite well. She had lots of friends and a few hobbies she enjoyed. Both Taylor and Hunter worked a lot, and their schedules often didn't mesh. They didn't see much of each other even though they lived together. She described their relationship as okay but not great. They functioned well together and had fun, but there was no real depth to the quality of the relationship. Their conversations were superficial. When Taylor thought about her future, she could not see marrying Hunter (even though she wanted to marry and have kids eventually), yet she saw no legitimate reason to break up with him. She also knew in her heart he would *never* leave her.

Taylor's parents had been divorced since she was eight years old. After the divorce, her mother had remarried four times, and her father had married a woman half his age. He had also spent some time in jail after committing a white-collar crime when she was a teenager. There had been little stability in her life with all these unreliable and inconsistent adults.

This is perhaps the reason Taylor stayed in the relationship with Hunter. She did not feel like she was in love with him, yet she simply could not dump a guy who was consistent, reliable, and a good person. She stayed in this no-man's-land with him year after year. Hunter was safe. He did not activate her attachment fears at all. He was a low risk emotionally. It wasn't necessarily wrong for her to stay with him. However, she was denying her need for romantic love and a deep connection. She was ignoring her dream of marriage and children. She was hiding out in this relationship, making sure she never got hurt. In fact, they both were hiding out.

Here are some typical signs that you may be avoiding intimacy:

- You believe there is only one true love, or soul mate, out there.
- You have a ridiculously long checklist that describes the type of person you would be willing to commit to.
- You sleep with a potential romantic partner very early in the relationship.
- You choose people who are geographically undesirable.
- You tend to drink a lot or get drunk on dates.
- You get very uncomfortable when asked questions you perceive as personal.
- You tend to engage only in superficial or lighthearted discussions.
- You can have a lot of fun with someone, but you don't want to deal with anything serious.
- You have no trouble working a lot or canceling dates for work-related obligations.
- You are likely very "put together" in a lot of ways and can be counted on.
- You can come on strong or be highly opinionated in a way that turns people off.
- You can be highly sensitive and, more specifically, you greatly fear criticism, disapproval, or rejection.
- You stay too long with the wrong person even after you realize it.

You Have a Propensity for Drama

You are addicted to the chase or to the chaotic nature of the relationship. The fantasy of the relationship's potential becomes more important than its reality. At the pinnacle of this type of relationship, you can be brought down to a sobering sense of reality. The allure fades, and the mundaneness of life sets in again.

This is the appeal of one-sided love for some people. If you prolong the pursuit, then you do not have to face the anticlimactic sense of coming down from the romantic high. It stimulates high drama, providing the ideal antidote to any boredom that may be lurking in other areas of your life.

I have heard several stories from women who found themselves in perpetual chaos. Peace and calm are given a bad rap — they're viewed as boring. Continual drama and chaos also bring attention and sometimes sympathy from others: "Oh, poor Abby, she has such bad luck with men!" But what's really going on with Abby?

Abby always felt like she had bad luck in relationships. She seemed to pick one bad guy after the other. Her last three dating interactions had gone like this: The first was with Noah. She fell head over heels for him instantly. She slept with him after the second date. When he didn't call her the next day, she went nuts, sending him a nasty text calling him a user and a jerk. She told all her friends the story and was incredulous that this guy could do this to her. She had so much trouble concentrating at work because of this situation that her boss took notice. He reprimanded her privately for her sloppy work that day. Then came Oliver to take her mind off of Noah. Right away, she thought he, too, was awesome and attractive. She waited a week to sleep with him. He did call her the day after but, from then on, rather inconsistently. This would upset Abby, but instead of talking to him about her feelings, she flirted heavily with a few exes that she was in touch with. One day, she "accidentally" slept with one of them after getting drunk. She swore she would never do that again, because she really liked Oliver. But, through the grapevine, Oliver found out and broke up with her. She was so beside herself that she was determined to find out who ratted on her and get revenge. She was even more angry that Oliver now blocked her on his phone and social media. She showed up at his apartment in the middle of the night and screamed obscenities through the closed front door (since he would not open it for her). The next day, she regretted this and cried to all her friends about how she had been treated by "everyone" lately. But she even got the vibe from them that they were sick of hearing about her bad luck.

Abby was comfortable in chaos. She had no blueprint for what peace or calm looks like. Her family had moved eight times while she was growing up because of her father's irresponsible behavior, and she often heard her parents fighting loudly while she was trying to sleep. Her mother finally gave up and divorced her father when she was twelve. A long, drawn-out battle over custody and finances ensued. Abby was often caught in a tug-of-war between her parents and would overhear the constant insults they hurled at each other. She spent more time with her friends or smoking pot to get away from it all.

Abby's behavior as an adult makes sense based on what we know about her history. However, we know this will not help her get what she truly wants and needs out of life: stability and a loving relationship. Until she recognizes that she is attracted to drama and the reasons why, she may not be able to carve out a more functional and healthy way of interacting.

Here are some signs that you are attracted to drama:

- You engage in behavior that regularly affects your ability to function (eat, sleep, go to work, and so on).

- You engage in behavior that regularly yields negative consequences.
- You think normalcy is boring.
- You feel like you can't stop your behavior even when a part of you knows it is harmful or illogical.
- You have trouble setting boundaries with others, and not just in romantic relationships.
- You often seem to have multiple crises going on and are never "crisis-free" for too long.
- You feel really good when the attention is on you or you get sympathetic responses from others.
- You quickly escalate, or emotionally break down, in an argument and/or engage others to take your "side" in a fight.
- You seem to be the common denominator in all your troubled relationships, including your relationships with family and friends.
- You feel like something is "off" when things are going too well or it's too calm in your life.
- You have a lot of trouble bouncing back when things don't go your way or your expectations are not met.
- You get off on gossip and can stir the pot when you are privy to a bad story about someone you know.
- Someone has already called you a "drama queen" or the like.

You Are Stuck in the Past

From time to time, you experience a fear of love that is likely rooted in your past involving painful experiences and disappointments. It can reflect the negative impact of sexual and/or emotional abuse. It can also be worsened by having an innate sensitivity to past troubling experiences. Any of these conditions has the potential to make you susceptible to typical interactions with unavailable men. Caught in this painful cycle, you may experience some amount of love or passion without being swept away by it. You can nurture your desires by always keeping yourself on the periphery of completely fulfilling them. But staying in the past will undoubtedly keep love out of your life today.

Chloe had a lot of trouble getting unstuck from what had happened to her in childhood. She had a horrible time after things drastically changed when she was around ten. Her father got terminal cancer, devastating the family. Her parents had always had what seemed to be a good marriage as far as she could tell. Her mother stepped up to take care of her father while he was sick and dying. Her father, whom she adored, started to get mean and hypercritical. This wasn't how he used to be. Her mother would tell her to "ignore" his words, that he was just unhappy about being sick and afraid to die. Soon, Chloe couldn't do anything right in his eyes. When he did pass away, Chloe thought she did not even deserve a father after being such a horrible daughter. She sank into a state of depression and was diagnosed with dysthymia. Her self-esteem was shattered, and she was pessimistic and felt down most of the time. She would sink into a deep depression whenever she felt criticized at work or by her friends. Some of them distanced themselves from her because she was always negative and complained a lot.

She thought things were better for her after meeting Ben. He made her laugh and feel important. After a few months in this relationship, she naturally felt comfortable enough to be herself. Yet "herself" was a lot of complaining and a lot of negativity. When Ben tried to address this with her, she would take the feedback very poorly and say something like "Just break up with me; I know I'm not good enough for you!" If Ben suggested she get some help for her "father issues," she would refuse, saying she could handle things on her own. Finally, Ben could not take it anymore and broke up with Chloe.

Chloe could not see that she was stuck in the past. She was a victim of terrible circumstances while growing up that were not her fault. But she clung to this victim mentality as an adult. This kind of negative energy will push those you love away as it did Ben.

Here are some typical signs that you are stuck in the past:

- You bitch and moan a lot.
- You resent the things that didn't go your way.
- People think you are negative, or you already know you are negative.
- You react poorly to feedback.
- You hang on to meaningless possessions (for example, clothing, cards, photos of exes) from the past.
- You have passed up many excellent opportunities that have come your way.
- You would rather suffer than ask for help.
- You hold grudges.
- You have been told you need to "move on."
- You don't seem to know what you really want.
- You have a lot of trouble making decisions.
- You still mention or focus on your exes a lot.
- You dwell on adverse events from your history, especially your childhood.

Your Defenses Are in Overdrive

According to many theorists, people use defense mechanisms to avoid difficult feelings and insecurity. Some defenses are actually helpful to us. They offer us a way to cope better when life gets tough. However, some defenses — like projection and denial, in particular — can sabotage our relationships. These defenses are unconscious and outside our awareness.

Projection is a term often used in psychology to describe how we tend to see things in another person that actually apply to ourselves. For instance, you believe your partner isn't caring enough when, in reality, maybe you are the one who isn't caring enough. Projections also operate more strongly when we are admiring a person from a distance. We don't yet see the flaws that would become more obvious if we were to live with the person day to day.

Denial is an extreme way to protect ourselves. We literally deny the reality of a situation: if I think it isn't happening, then it really isn't happening. This way, it doesn't enter conscious thought, and we get to circumvent anxious feelings. For example, when someone you love is unhappy with you, it is easy to just pretend everything will magically be okay, and you get to avoid dealing with it directly.

One other concept encompassed in defensive strategies is called *repetition compulsion*. This is when you repeat your negative past circumstances over and over again throughout your life in an attempt to rewrite history. This can include reenacting a circumstance or putting yourself in situations where the same outcome is likely to happen again. The intention is to finally work through the traumatic situation. As you probably guessed, it is often the parent/child relationship you are attempting to resolve.

Gina's defenses were hard at work in her relationship choices. She had a deep-seated feeling of rejection by both of her parents. They had had a "children should be seen and not heard" type of attitude. She was an only child and the result of an unplanned pregnancy. She would make multiple attempts to engage her parents and get their attention. Sometimes it would work, but it never lasted.

Gina's situation was a typical repetition-compulsion scenario. She frequently picked men who gave her little attention. She would also make repeated attempts to change this dynamic. She would dress sexy for them, cook meals, send them love notes, and do other sweet things. Her efforts never resulted in her feeling fully connected to these men and often made her feel the familiar sense of rejection. Her denial kept her from seeing that she was picking men who were incapable of connecting with her. She was repeating the same dynamic in her family over and over and, sure enough, getting the same results!

These defenses can be cunning and powerful. They are beyond frustrating to those around you, as well. Most critically, if you will stop sabotaging yourself you will have a real chance at finding love. Let's take a look at some signs that your defenses are in overdrive.

Signs that you are projecting:

- You don't admit your flaws.
- You have trouble admitting when you are wrong.
- You think many of those around you do not like you.
- You feel discomfort in social situations.
- You can react really strongly to things that don't tend to bother anyone else.
- You accuse your partner of cheating or being untrustworthy, with little evidence to back it up.
- You quickly focus on the flaws of others, especially those of your partner.
- Others describe *you* in the same way that you negatively describe your partner.

Signs that you are in denial:

- You try to control the uncontrollable.
- You ignore or minimize problems, thinking they will go away on their own.
- You tend to be secretive.
- You don't want to hear the opinions of others.
- You keep a lot of "yes-men" around you, so you aren't challenged by someone else's feedback or critique of your behavior.
- You are rigid about making changes or trying something new or different.
- You often act like you don't care.
- You don't like to seek help, even when things are falling apart.
- You get defensive or angry at anyone who expresses concern about you or your relationship.
- You focus the most on the rare good times, rather than on all the bad things in your relationship, to avoid dealing with the truth.

Signs that you are stuck in repetition compulsion:

- You have a habit of picking partners similar your father.
- Your partner's similarities to that parent are his shortcomings or dysfunctional behaviors.
- You believe you can fix your partner's deficits.
- You seem to be repeating the same type of interactions in your relationship that you saw in your parents' relationship.

Finding ways to become conscious of these defenses is critical to your ability to stop engaging in them. Such insight will also enable you to finally face the feelings that come with the reality of a less-than-perfect childhood. Getting unstuck and consciously accepting your past will help you make better relationship choices in the future.

You Have Trouble Being Alone

If you have a lot of trouble being alone, you will go to great lengths to avoid it. *Somebody* is better than *nobody*. Being physically alone readily creates the feeling of loneliness for you. And the feeling of loneliness is dreadful. When this happens, you may end up with unsuitable partners, or you may stay too long with the wrong one. You might go overboard trying to please your man or mold yourself into what he wants you to be so that he won't ever leave.

This fear of loneliness is a surefire way to tolerate bad behavior in romantic partners. As long as you have a "warm body," you are okay. However, it is another way for you to keep yourself from having the love in your life that you deserve. This is probably one of the most common reasons that people stay in a relationship with someone who mistreats them, and chapter 8 thoroughly addresses this topic.

Signs that you have trouble being alone:

- You equate being single with being pathetic or horrible.
- You quickly feel depressed when alone.
- You have a lot of discomfort when doing things by yourself.
- Being alone triggers anxiety and fear.
- You go to great lengths not to lose a relationship.
- You worry a lot about what others think of you.
- You tend to mistrust others.

You Believe Your Love Will Fix Him

When a woman thinks her love will be the cure to her partner's reasons for being emotionally unavailable, she is pouring her heart and soul into a fantasy. There was an especially popular bestseller written in 1985 by Robin Norwood titled *Women Who Love Too Much: When You Keep Wishing and Hoping He'll Change*. The author's premise is that women are chasing after the love they didn't get from a parent. In essence, these women experience a transference: they redirect their need for love, safety, and affection to men, and they do so in a compulsive or addictive way. But as you probably can guess, these women are never fulfilled in these relationships with incapable men.

Norwood's book outlines an addiction/codependency model that might resonate with you and might apply to you, but not to all women in such relationships. If the addiction model is correct, which indeed is possible, then a woman can become addicted to another person. If we further consider the addiction model, we know that part of addiction includes the consequences of the addictive behavior. To figure out if you have an addiction, ask yourself about the consequences you are suffering. What are they? Are they all negative? Are you getting anything positive from your behavior? My guess is that your behavior prolongs your pain and suffering. You are not entirely to blame for what happens between you and men — we can also look at culture, society, gender norms, and so on. Suffice it to say that believing you have the power to change someone through love — or any other means, for that matter — is not going to help you. The cliché is true: you can't change anyone but yourself.

Signs that you think your love will fix him:

- During your childhood, one or both parents were emotionally or physically unavailable or had a substance abuse problem.
- You are generally controlling.
- You are in a helping profession.
- You immediately blame yourself for your problems, even things that are beyond your control.
- You feel compulsive about changing a man who is cold, unresponsive, unloving, or unkind.
- You feel like you can't control your behavior when it comes to relationships.
- You would say that you are obsessed with your love interest.
- You regularly think about ways you can finally get your needs met in a relationship.
- Sometimes, you believe you have to manipulate others to get your needs met.
- You feel a sense of powerlessness over your ability to stop repeating your patterns with men.

You Feel Very Bad about Yourself

Feeling bad about yourself is also known as low self-esteem. When you have low self-esteem, you feel a lack of confidence, or you feel unworthy, incapable, or incompetent. You may even feel unlovable or that you deserve to be treated poorly. Furthermore, feeling this way about yourself will prolong your poor self-esteem. You will make life choices, including relationship choices, that come from this negative self-concept.

You may not be *attracting* the wrong men, but, because you don't value yourself, you are readily *accepting* the wrong men. If you don't know your worth, how can someone else?

Feeling better about yourself comes only from taking action despite how you feel about yourself. It's about taking risks and chances in the face of fear or thinking you will fail, and doing so regardless of the negative voice in your head. If you don't step out of your comfort zone, you will continue to create these destructive self-fulfilling prophecies.

Signs that you feel bad about yourself:

- You came from a family that made you believe you were never good enough, or you endured a lot of criticism.
- You believe a good relationship will help you feel the way you want.
- You don't believe anyone could really love you.
- When you look in the mirror, you think you are unattractive and/or fat.
- You don't think you are smart.
- You have much difficulty celebrating your achievements.
- You have difficulty listing your strengths or positive attributes.
- You believe no one could love you if they knew the real you.
- You put up with being treated poorly by a man because it is better than having no man at all.
- You are guarded when it comes to self-disclosure.
- You frequently apologize, even when you aren't sure you did something wrong.
- You have been called needy or clingy by others.
- You are excessively sensitive to rejection and criticism.
- You are a people pleaser and have trouble saying no or making decisions.

- You go way overboard in spending time and money on your appearance and clothing — or the opposite: you don't do anything about your appearance.
- You abandon your dreams and goals to accommodate your partner(s).

You Want What You Can't Have

When we can't have what we desire, we want it more. When we get bits and pieces ("breadcrumbs") once in a while, we want it even more than when we can't have it at all. The highs and lows of an unpredictable romantic interest put us on what is known in the world of behaviorism and learning as an "intermittent reinforcement schedule." This schedule is likely to elicit a response from you because you never know when the reward will come. The reward (his attention) sometimes comes after your pursuit and protest behaviors, but not every time. A good example of an intermittent reinforcement schedule, in another context, is playing slot machines in a casino. Many people get hooked on the game because they know that the more they play, the more likely they are to finally get the reward at some point.

You Have an Untreated Mental Health Problem

Could an untreated mental health problem be wreaking havoc on your love life? You may not realize that some of the symptoms you are experiencing might be those of clinical depression, an anxiety disorder, bipolar disorder, chemical addiction, trauma, or a personality disorder. You may have a mental disorder and an addiction coexisting along with some of the other concerns discussed in this chapter. It's not as unusual as you might think.

If you are being treated poorly, your love is not reciprocated, or the man has directly told you he doesn't want you in his life, but you persist in getting, or attempting to get, what you want anyway, you may have developed a romantic obsession. If your behavior consists of ongoing invasive or unwanted pursuit, this is even more troublesome. If the pursuit ignites fear in the target of such behavior, it may have risen to the level of stalking. This is going way too far and may indicate an underlying mental health condition or personality disorder. Continuing such actions may even land you in legal trouble.

Symptoms of a mental disorder can become activated within the context of a romantic relationship. This does not necessarily mean the relationship is the cause of the disorder, but it may very well exacerbate an underlying problem. Furthermore, if the diagnosis is known to have a biological basis, you may get better only with medication.

I cannot provide a comprehensive list, within this book, of the mental disorders that could be affecting you, because there are too many possibilities. If you think you have a mental health disorder, you will get an accurate diagnosis only by seeing a licensed mental health professional. From there, a treatment plan will be developed to address the specific diagnosis and any other concerns, including relational, that you have as well. Chapter 12 discusses getting help in more detail.

If you genuinely desire a committed relationship, bear in mind that it will not materialize unless you and another person have the *same* feelings at the *same* time. It is imperative to take a look at yourself to discover what is holding you back from finding love. A good place to begin is to think about your early family-of-origin patterns. These early patterns are profoundly implicated in the underlying reasons why you do what you do when it comes to romantic relationships.

CHAPTER FIVE

THE IMPACT OF YOUR FAMILY HISTORY

Your family of origin (FOO) — meaning the family you grew up in — has shaped and formed the person you have become. From your FOO (and through intergenerational influences) you learned many critical elements of life that affect you daily: how to communicate, how to make sense of and process emotions, and how to get your needs met, among others. Within your family, you also formulated your values and your beliefs about yourself and the world. It is not surprising, then, that your FOO has a significant impact on your love life.

As noted in the brief overview of attachment patterns in chapter 2, such patterns play a core role in the romantic choices of both men and women. A deeper look at attachment concepts and the part they play in your love life will be useful to you. But we also must consider adverse events you may have been exposed to, including abuse, trauma, health problems, divorce, or poverty. Intentionally or not, echoes of your FOO are an undercurrent of your life and are most powerful in your friendships and romantic relationships. It is common for people to develop certain expectations for a romantic partner, who may be unaware, unable, or unwilling to fulfill them. Therefore, to wholly understand your beliefs and behaviors in adult relationships, it is necessary to investigate *why* and *how* those beliefs and behaviors first developed.

There are several ways you can start to understand your family and childhood history. The process is complex and should shift you from simply not understanding your family and history to engaging in the process of changing what you now understand. When you go from insight to behavioral change in your life and relationships, you will fulfill your goals in these areas as well.

I recommend that you journal and/or meet with a therapist as you explore your FOO. Emotional triggers are likely to arise. It helps to have a therapist or, at the very least, a close, trusted friend to offer support. Licensed marriage and family therapists have training in family dynamics and can help you if you decide to try therapy. The focus of your FOO exploration is on your relationship patterns and partner choices. Keep this in the forefront of your mind as the purpose, and reason, for what you are doing. As you read this chapter, ask yourself a key question: How do I think these concepts influence my relationship choices?

Family Rules and Boundaries

When it comes to family structure and boundaries, much of what we know comes from the work of a psychologist named Salvador Minuchin. He expounded the idea that a family's structure is essentially the unspoken set of rules and demands that establishes the ways in which family members interact with each other. The unspoken, or invisible, part of this family structure is emphasized because it characterizes most of the relational and communicative exchanges within a family. You should note that these rules are not always dysfunctional or pathological. They exist on a continuum from healthy to unhealthy. For example, you know never to mention Uncle Joe (your mom's horrible brother), you know who gets invited (and excluded) from holiday parties, and you know which parent to ask if you are looking for a "yes" to your request. These hidden rules can carry a good deal of power in a family's daily interactions. If unhealthy, they can cause significant problems in adulthood. Extreme examples include unspoken rules and secrets concerning physical, sexual, and emotional abuse, as well as issues of neglect and substance abuse in a family.

The heart of a family's organization is determined by its boundaries. Boundaries are about the interactions among family members and who is or is not allowed into the family system. Boundaries are also influenced by who is aligned with whom, such as father-son or mother-daughter allies. Which person in the family has the most power is also a matter of importance. How clear or muddied the boundaries are can determine the level of function or dysfunction within the family.

When thinking about your family, what do you remember about the boundaries between your parents, siblings, extended family, and strangers? These boundaries exist on a range and include *clear*, *disengaged*, and *enmeshed*.

- **Clear:** The hierarchy of authority and responsibility is clearly and explicitly communicated and understood. Clear boundaries help children develop self-control, function well in society, and feel cared for and safe

within the family. Clear boundaries are healthy boundaries.

- **Disengaged:** These boundaries are not directly communicated. It is implied that certain lines of responsibility or authority are strictly enforced and must be
followed. In these types of families, children have limited access to parents. The expression of feelings and
needs is stifled. Interdependence is not encouraged
between family members, and independence is heavily valued.

- **Enmeshed:** In these families, the positions of who is
in charge and who is responsible for what are fuzzy.
There is often communication among family members
that crosses the line of appropriateness — for instance,
a mother leans on her daughter for support for her
marital problems. In these families, independence and
individuality are discouraged. Parents may have a tremendous amount of trouble cutting the apron strings,
remaining overinvolved well into adulthood.

When Janet reflects on her family, she believes the
boundaries were disengaged. Her parents strike her as very
"old-fashioned." Her father was the breadwinner, and her
mother was a housewife. They both showed little physical affection for Janet. But her mother would dote on her father,
and they seemed happy together, from Janet's perspective.
Her mother had trouble disciplining Janet and her brother.
She would say, "Wait until your father gets home from work!"
When he did, there was never any discussion, just harsh and
sometimes physical punishment. Janet does not remember
much of her childhood. There weren't many family vacations,
but her parents went away together often. Her parents also did

not speak openly about the facts of life, leaving her to discover this information on her own or through friends.

Tina, on the other hand, believes that in her family the boundaries were both enmeshed and unclear. By enmeshed, I mean that it seemed her parents were always in her business and she had no privacy. She was expected to disclose anything and everything about her life to her parents. It seemed nothing was off-limits. She remembers being horrified that her brother found and read her private diary when she was a teenager, and that her parents brushed it off. She also remembers her mother embarrassing her at times by trying to "hang out" with her girlfriends and dressing in clothes similar to what Tina wore. Her mother became hysterical when she learned that Tina was going to go to college in another state after high school graduation. Tina felt so guilty that she changed her plans and went to a community college nearby — something she always regretted.

Family Communication

When you reflect upon your FOO, what is your impression of how information about needs, feelings, problems, rules, and so on were communicated? When communication is direct, it is conveyed clearly and understood without room for misinterpretation. If the communication was indirect, your parents likely did not express their feelings in a clear and forthcoming manner. Instead, they may have used criticism, sarcasm, disapproving looks, jokes, or silence to express themselves to you. They also might have not responded well to your attempts at direct communication.

These are some ways your parents may have taught you poor communication:

- **Communicating through a third party, such as a sibling or another family member:** This is called *triangulation*. A parent may use the children in a way that inhibits direct communication between spouses. For example, a parent complains to his or her child about the spouse's behavior instead of directly discussing it with the spouse. A parent may also triangulate the marriage by drawing another family member or a third party into the discussion. This could be a grandparent or a secret affair partner.

- **Treating a child as if he or she does not have a voice in the family:** The child is treated as "less than." His or her feelings and ideas go ignored, or they are negated, minimized, or quickly shut down. In some instances, the child is not entitled to have, express, or experience feelings deemed unacceptable to the parents.

- **Ignoring the elephant in the room:** This happens when a major problem is not spoken of, such as sexual abuse or addiction within the family.

- **Constantly expressing negative feelings:** Negative feelings and emotions are readily expressed, instead of positive ones. Or there is a lack of physical affection and warmth.

- **Setting and enforcing boundaries that can be broken at any time:** Some parents set boundaries that they don't model themselves. Furthermore, they show inconsistency in the enforcement of boundaries.

- **Keeping secrets that are not allowed to be shared outside the family circle:** These secrets are typically about something embarrassing, unorthodox, or abusive.

- **Making the children take on adult responsibilities:** When a child becomes *parentified*, he or she either takes on adult responsibilities or is expected to meet his or her parents' emotional needs. This frequently occurs when the parents are addicts or are irresponsible or emotionally absent. The child's emotional needs are neglected.

- **Lacking respect for a child's personal boundaries, which include his or her body, the physical space around it, and/ or his or her general privacy:** This may run the gamut from inappropriate behavior to the most extreme instance of sexual abuse.

- **Failing to resolve problems:** Ongoing problems or concerns continue to loom, causing stress and conflict among family members that never seem to get resolved.

- **Neglecting to process a loss or crisis:** This occurs when there is a major crisis or loss and the parents do not help the child make sense of it. For example, a family member dies suddenly, the parents divorce, or the family moves to a new area and no one checks in with the child to discuss his or her thoughts and feelings about the event.

- **Being excessively punitive and controlling:** These parents are highly demanding and not tolerant of mistakes. They don't strike enough of a balance between being controlling and allowing their children's independence. Or the parents have difficulty seeing their children as separate individuals.

These faulty communication patterns can also influence us in a covert, or unconscious, way. We may not realize that how we communicate in all our social relationships is influenced by the communication we experienced or saw modeled for us. But as an adult, you can now choose which patterns you want to either change or perpetuate.

Childhood Abuse or Neglect and Domestic Violence

Nothing would likely have influenced you more than if you experienced emotional, physical, or sexual abuse in your childhood — likewise if you were subjected to extreme neglect or witnessed domestic violence. These experiences go beyond negative or faulty communication patterns and tremendously affect your sense of safety in the world and with others.

Kelsey did not quite realize she had been abused until she got into therapy for depression in her thirties. She thought her depression was a result of numerous relationship failures. She also noticed she was always suspicious of people's motives. Even if someone was genuinely nice, she could not believe it. She had trouble accepting compliments and thought that she was to blame for anything that went wrong in her personal life and at work.

After "peeling back several layers of the onion," Kelsey discovered she was a victim of childhood emotional abuse. Her parents had often shamed and humiliated her, teased her until she was in tears, constantly reminded her of her short-comings, and punished her for the smallest infractions. She believed this was normal parenting until her eyes opened wide during therapy. She was able to connect the dots between this abuse and her behavior as an adult. The typical man she would pick was narcissistic. Kelsey was the perfect target for his manipulations and was made a scapegoat for everything that wasn't going right in the relationship.

On the other end of the spectrum is Denise. She was a victim of neglect in her family. As an adult, she often felt a sense of "not belonging." She would describe herself as "emotionally hollow." She had difficulty identifying her feelings, and if anyone asked how she was doing, she would always say "fine" regardless of what was happening in her life. Denise had a knack for picking men who were alcoholics, workaholics, and porn addicts.

Denise's mother had passed away from cancer when she was only six. She had only a handful of memories of her mother. Her father was a functional alcoholic who got much worse after her mother died. He worked a nine-to-five job and, most nights, would come home and sit on the couch and drink. He was emotionally checked out and did the minimum to care for Denise. He would certainly take her to the doctor if she was sick, but he didn't do much else. Denise had to get herself dressed for school, pack her own lunch, and make dinner for herself most evenings. In high school, she spent a lot of time at the homes of her friends or a boyfriend. She felt like she had lots of freedom to do whatever she wanted with minimal rules.

Some signs of abuse are obvious, such as being physically harmed or sexually abused. But some are subtle. Either way, the result is often an extremely negative view of oneself and a deep sense of unworthiness, and it is extremely common to find oneself continually a victim of abuse in romantic relationships. I highly recommend that you seek professional guidance if you grew up in an abusive household.

Divorce

If your parents divorced, then, most likely, you experienced a significantly traumatic event in your childhood. Regardless of how well your parents handled the divorce, you were left with some lingering effects. Like other family problems, divorce can perpetuate itself for generations to come. The divorce rate is still around 50 percent for all first marriages. There exists an attitude that divorce is a viable solution to relationship problems. There is also much less stigma associated with divorce than there was a few decades ago.

If you are an adult child of divorced parents, you might find yourself less optimistic about your ability to have a successful marriage and may even avoid such a commitment altogether. Your overall quality of life, sense of well-being, and ability to navigate relational conflict are also compromised. You are not doomed to repeat this outcome if you decide to commit to someone. But you may have to take extra precautions to make certain you don't succumb to the impact your parents' divorce has had on you.

Addiction

The residual consequences of having an addict as a parent are something you should examine. One can be addicted to a substance, food, gambling, eating, and so on. If one of your parents was an addict, you have seen a parent lose his or her ability to control a destructive or unhealthy behavior.

As an adult child of an addict or alcoholic, you may also have significant issues relating to control: the fear of losing control and an inclination to control others. Other characteristics include a constant desire for approval, sensitivity to criticism, difficulty relaxing or having fun, an affinity for chaos, and a tendency to develop one's own addictions. When it comes to intimacy, you may repeat this pattern by pairing up with an addict or someone you feel the need to rescue. Becoming a codependent (an enabler) is a serious concern.

I strongly recommend that you develop a comprehensive understanding of the influence of an addicted or alcoholic parent by reading some of the books on this topic. I have included some recommendations in the Recommended Resources (page 209).

Abandonment

Physical abandonment can profoundly influence a child's future love life. An absent father is particularly influential in a daughter's negative romantic partner choices. Having at least one stable and consistent caregiver can significantly diminish the negative impacts of one parent's abandonment. But if this is not your circumstance, it's possible you have a very deep wound that has created a toxic level of shame. You constantly worry about being rejected and abandoned again — so much so that, ironically, you re-create this circumstance in your life through your own erratic and inconsistent behavior or a compulsive attraction to those who are already unavailable. In some instances, if the emotions are intense, the individual may develop an anxiety disorder or personality disorder.

Attachment Theory Revisited

Remember that attachment theory emphasizes the basic need for security in close relationships. The above descriptions show how communication patterns, boundaries, and so on may have affected the sense of security you had growing up in your FOO household. We use attachment theory to describe the deeper roots of the parent-child relationship because it has been proven that these patterns are reactivated in adult romantic relationships.

One of the beneficial aspects of attachment theory is that it normalizes many of the behaviors that are exhibited in a romantic relationship. For example, if you grew up with your feelings constantly shut down and negated, how could you know to behave any differently as an adult? How could you possibly feel safe to express yourself when no one ever made it safe for you? Attachment theory also destigmatizes the concept of dependency. We need others in order to survive. Where the struggle lies is when the dependency is not equal and reciprocal. A mutual, back-and-forth relationship is also termed *effective dependency*. Members of a couple must depend on and express needs to *each other*. It is not just one-sided (that's *codependency*). It is also not about never needing anyone (that's *coexisting*). When two people are interdependent on each other, a healthy, loving relationship flourishes.

To reiterate something I discussed in chapter 2, three insecure attachment styles are *anxious, avoidant*, and *disorganized*. The *anxious attachment style* often arises out of having an inconsistent caregiver, usually a parent, in childhood. The *avoidant attachment style* usually arises from having a predominantly unavailable caregiver. Finally, the *disorganized attachment style* is frequently a result of childhood abuse, trauma, or severe inconsistency in parenting. In this style, the attachment figure (the person you are supposed to be able to go to for safety) is also the source of distress. This may result in extreme reactions, such as *dissociation*, in order to cope.

The family rules, boundaries, structure, and communication patterns all help determine the security of your attachment. Secure attachment results from clear boundaries, appropriate rules and discipline, consistency, and predictability within the family. Attachment is formed within your FOO and your life experiences that occur both within and outside of your family.

If you find yourself repeatedly in relationships with unavailable men (usually the avoidant style), there is a high probability that you have the anxious or disorganized style of attachment. Your actions and responses to others will mirror the patterns established while you were growing up. There is constant preoccupation with the relationship and worry about being loved. A pattern that emerges when an anxious style and avoidant style link up is the one most commonly seen in couples' therapy. In adult relationships, it is called a *pursue* (or *demand*)/*withdraw pattern*, where the anxious partner relentlessly pursues connection with the avoidant partner. A vicious cycle ensues over the battle for closeness and distance, with the pursuer escalating his or her attempts to connect (and feel safe), triggering the avoidant partner to avoid even more.

Growing up in a household with toxic communication patterns, poor treatment, and traumatic experiences can cause a lot of confusion and challenges in your adult relationships. You may find yourself unreasonably guarded, easily defensive, and even suspicious in your interactions. You may find it tough to open up, express yourself, or make decisions. You may have trouble with the emotional cues and signals given off by others. Above all, these communication patterns give rise to self-doubt, which makes a lot of sense when it comes to your interactions with unavailable men. If you are used to unclear signals, this is your "normal."

As you reflect upon your FOO experiences, it is natural to feel uncomfortable. You may wish to protect your family or rationalize what you are reading — for instance, thinking "they did the best they could" or "there are parents who were even worse." Even if these statements are true, however, it is still imperative that you focus on your perceptions and the impact of your FOO experiences. You can also offer yourself nonjudgmental acceptance and empathy for what you have endured. Once you do so, you are likely to be able to understand each of your family members better. It is your choice to forgive as well, if you believe that is helpful.

CHAPTER SIX

BUT I'M IN LOVE

People are fascinated by love. One of the most popular searches on Google is the question "What is love?" Science has helped answer this question, but I'm not sure we will ever know the entire answer. One thing most will agree upon is that the experience of being in love is one of the best feelings in the world. We spend a significant amount of time thinking about how love makes us feel, whether good, bad, safe, secure, strong, vulnerable, or distressed. Whatever it makes us feel, love is a powerful experience that has a significant impact throughout our lives. We strive to understand love and be successful in love, which may be more achievable than most people think.

Some people might view the topic of love as a waste of time. I can tell you, without doubt, that it is in no way whatsoever a waste. We thrive when our relationships with the people we love — our spouses, our children, our best friends — are going well, and we are in distress when they aren't. Loving relationships are crucial for our survival and our well-being, starting at birth. Our need for love never dissipates. For many, a relationship with one other person is the only means of a loving and emotional connection. Others live in social isolation, which has now become epidemic. Given the importance of love, it's important to discuss how to understand it, get it, and sustain it.

Attachment Is the Foundation of Love

Attachment begins at birth, and we experience it throughout our lives — from the cradle to the grave. When we fall in love, we are creating a new attachment in our lives, one that we will maintain by actively engaging in loving, caring, and affectionate behaviors. How such behaviors were modeled for you will profoundly influence your choice of romantic partners in adulthood.

Several core components make up attachment. First, we use a "preferred person," such as our mother, as a secure base while we explore the world and as a haven for comfort and safety when needed. Second, we feel most secure when we know this person will be consistent, responsive, and available to help when we seek it. In other words, this individual will be there for you. Ironically, the more connected we feel on this level, the more autonomous, or independent, we can also be. Third, we feel insecure when we do not believe this person will always be there or respond to our signs of distress. Furthermore, if his or her care has been inconsistent or absent, extreme anxiety can arise when we are not in the presence of this loved one. Moreover, a sense of safety and security when we are by ourselves is missing. There is an intrinsic need to be attached and close to a few beloved people that continues throughout our life span.

Attachment and Mature Love

Other researchers expanded upon Bowlby's groundbreaking work by looking at adult romantic relationships through the attachment lens. With mounting evidence in support of attachment concepts in adulthood, Dr. Sue Johnson developed a model for working with couples called emotionally focused couples' therapy. A central tenet of this therapy is that, when two partners feel secure, they can reach out to each other and connect, readily helping each other find emotional equilibrium. On the contrary, when they feel insecure, they become either critical, angry, and demanding or shut down and distant. In this therapy, couples' interactions are predictable patterns that result from relationship distress. Needing others is not viewed as weak. Furthermore, the nurturing of mutual dependency — in essence, an interdependency — with one primary person (usually a romantic partner) is necessary for us to survive and thrive.

What about the circumstance of a troubled childhood-attachment history? This most often leads to one of the "insecure" styles described in previous chapters. These insecure styles trigger avoidance, desperate closeness-seeking, or a combination of the two. Neither creates a peaceful and loved feeling! However, there is some flexibility in people's reactions, depending upon the situation or the object of affection.

Given what we are discussing in this book, we can focus on the fact that those who are avoidant tend to deny their longings for connection. They see others as perhaps dangerous or unreliable. In intimate and close relationships, this attitude comes off as disinterest. In turn, this predictably triggers an anxious reaction in the partner. If you are the partner of one of these people, then you have at times cranked up your attempts at connection, inadvertently contributing to an ongoing negative pattern of interaction between the two of you. To put it simply, the more he pulled away, the more you tried to reel him in — which, in turn, made him pull away even more; and on and on you both went in an anguished, self-defeating pattern.

Most typically, two secure people link up and create a stable and satisfying relationship. However, as previously mentioned, it is also commonplace for someone with an anxious attachment style to pair up with someone who has an avoidant attachment style. A relationship like this can survive on some level if the styles are not at the extreme ends of the continuum and each partner is fairly open to being influenced by the other. However, if the styles are extreme and entrenched, a highly distressed and unsatisfying relationship often ensues. Therefore, finding the right match for you is crucial. Falling in love with someone open to both receiving and giving love can give both of you a chance at creating a secure, happy, and long-lasting relationship.

Let's look at Dana's situation. She remembers feeling like the apple of her father's eye. He often doted on her and made her feel special. She was close to her mother, but her bond with her father seemed more special. She was shocked when her parents announced, while she was still a preteen, that they were divorcing. She would hear them fight on occasion, mostly about her mother being upset at her father's behavior. Her mother would often accuse him of lying. After the divorce, Dana learned things about her dad that confused her. She discovered that her father had had several affairs during the marriage, and that he was no longer someone she could rely on. A few times, he made a lame excuse not to see her, and she later found out that he went on a date instead. As Dana entered adulthood, she began to feel that she could not trust men at all. When dating, she constantly felt suspicious and could not relax and enjoy herself. With this behavior, she sabotaged a few relationships. She also picked a few cheaters along the way.

Everything turned around when Dana met Jim. He understood where she was coming from, because he had a few bad childhood stories of his own. Together, they made special attempts to make each other feel safe and secure. They were consistent with each other, always called when they said they would, and shared a lot of their personal stories. They transformed their attachment style — from insecure to secure — through good communication and by taking emotional risks with each other. This process is often called *earned security*, because it is accomplished at a later time in life, such as adulthood, with someone other than whoever was the primary caregiver during the early years.

Having a basic understanding of attachment helps us know why we act the way we do in dating and relationships. When you sense a romantic interest is pulling away from you, your tendency might be to seek him out more and to act clingy or needy, even desperate. Learning to identify what you feel inside and directly relay it to a partner is essential. This is called *emotional fluency*, and it is about being able to effectively put words to and express your emotions. Unless your partner responds to you early when you express yourself in this way, and before you reach the desperation level, you will be left feeling hurt, alone, and abandoned. If your partner does not respond kindly or ignores you, you must accept that he won't or can't, and it's not your job to teach him or change him. It is your responsibility to tune in to your own thoughts and feelings and pay attention to whether this person can respond with empathy to your emotional needs.

Love and Emotion

If you think about being in love, or you know someone in love, you also know the broad range of emotions most people use to describe being in love. Being in love brings amazing highs that are comparable to being on drugs and, at times, devastating lows when it isn't going so well. One emotion that you may not readily think of when it comes to love is fear. When we sense something dangerous or threatening, our alarms go off, warning us to spring into action. This is why you may get into a heightened state of fear, even panic, when you perceive you are disconnected, ignored, or rejected. You may get angry, but fear is often the underlying culprit. The fear-based reactions make more sense than many of us realize. They are adaptive and evolutionary, because they helped us survive as a species. Those same fear responses exist within us today.

The Chemistry of Love

Several chemicals in the body and brain, including hormones and neurotransmitters, make up the neurochemical feeling of love. Two primary parts of love influence attraction and the attachment system, and each of these involves a different chemical cocktail. Certain areas of the brain light up when you are experiencing love in its various stages.

The brain is split into a left and a right hemisphere, each having different functions. The right hemisphere is the seat of feelings, creativity, imagination, and holistic thinking. The left hemisphere is the seat of logic, reasoning, planning, and analytic thought. It is believed that the right hemisphere is the seat of love.

Brain-imaging studies tell us that two main areas of the brain become active when someone experiences romantic love. The first is made up of the foci in the media insula (also associated with instinct), and the other is the anterior cingulate cortex, which produces euphoric feelings. Together, these brain areas are responsible for making the feeling of being in love a happy and natural thing. In the earlier stages of love, other brain areas become active. These areas become flooded with dopamine, which is what makes love feel like being high. Dopamine is also referred to as the "love drug," because it can seem addictive.

The early stages of love are filled with infatuation, lust, and desire. Lust is regulated by our primary sex hormones, estrogen and testosterone. Desire involves our entire bodies, because it produces a surge of adrenaline (epinephrine), the same chemical involved in the fight-or-flight response. A similar physiological reaction takes place that increases the heart rate and alertness, dilates the pupils, and stimulates the sweat glands.

The experience of romantic love is accompanied by an increase in three central neurotransmitters: serotonin, dopamine, and norepinephrine. Our serotonin level surges, influencing feelings of infatuation. Dopamine is released as well, influencing the integration of emotion and thinking and stimulating the hypothalamus to release sex hormones. Dopamine is also triggered by excitement, novelty, and risk-taking. Dopamine and norepinephrine together produce euphoric and addictive feelings.

After the initial falling-in-love stage, people start to feel more relaxed and comfortable in the presence of their partners. When the relationship has more stability, other brain chemicals, such as oxytocin and vasopressin, begin to take over. Oxytocin, also named the "cuddle hormone," is released after sex and physical affection and is involved in feelings of closeness and intimacy. Oxytocin is released through touch such as kissing, stroking, and hugging. It is also released when we talk to our partners, which is why communication is critical to the long-term success of a relationship. In fact, oxytocin is fundamental to sustaining lifelong romantic attachments. Vasopressin, also known as the "monogamy hormone," influences couples to be faithful to one another. Animal studies have demonstrated that inhibiting vasopressin causes couples to become less devoted to one another.

There is little doubt that love is a biologically driven emotion. The composition of these different chemicals varies depending on which relationship phase someone is currently experiencing. The feel-good chemicals, like serotonin and dopamine, dominate the earlier stages; and in the later stages of deeper love within a relationship, which are characterized by bonding, intimacy, and often monogamy, the brain releases oxytocin and vasopressin. Love is a highly complex topic, yet science gives us a lot of useful information about it and about how long-lasting and genuinely loving relationships are sustained over the long term.

You don't have to remember the specific names of all these neurochemicals involved in love. However, it would be wise to be aware of what is happening inside you. You need to remind yourself that you may not be thinking as rationally and logically as you normally would if these chemicals were not swirling around in your system. Staying as grounded as possible will help you make smarter relationship choices.

Falling in Love

The early stages of love involve attraction, infatuation, lust, and sometimes even obsession. Feeling some degree of anxiety and fear in the beginning is natural. When we have attraction and some chemistry, we yearn for more. We want some affirmation that the object of our attraction has mutual feelings! We look for signs and signals all the time to affirm this mutuality and avoid potential rejection. We can become worried and sad when we don't get it. We often make every attempt to bring our "best selves" to those who attract us. When you get affirmation from someone that the feelings are mutual, this person becomes special to you. Soon, you both may take more emotional risks with each other and fall in love. If all goes well, you will gradually build a reciprocal, trusting, and secure bond.

There is not a whole lot of agreement about what causes someone to be sexually attracted to one person and not another. It is also highly unlikely that you'll develop an attraction to a specific person if you didn't do so at the start. Attraction has roots in evolution and our survival as a species. In this sense, it involves some degree of familiarity, smell, fertility in women and masculinity in men, and personality traits. Some traits are more universally desirable — for example, facial symmetry. But the most relevant part is that attraction is an individualized and unique experience.

The initial stage of love is termed *limerence*, and certain physical and psychological symptoms characterize this phase. Some of the physical symptoms are a racing heart, blushing, trembling, and heart palpitations. Some of the psychological symptoms are obsessive thoughts, excitement, fantasy, and fears of rejection. Various hormones, chemicals, and neurotransmitters are set off. But as you likely well know, this does not happen with just anyone! When it does happen, a torrent of symptoms and feelings comes flooding in. Unfortunately, along with these fantastic feelings come poor judgment and irrational thought — a double-edged sword, to say the least. When a person's judgment is poor and red flags are ignored, the next phase of love, called the *trust-building phase*, will be marred by extreme difficulty and frustration.

What happens when you don't get signals in return? What happens when you begin to realize that you can't count on the person you have such strong feelings for? You may pull away yourself and take your efforts elsewhere. This may be an excellent idea, since we know you will not always have your feelings returned. But you may decide, instead, to try even harder to reach your goal of having a successful relationship with the object of your affection. In this circumstance, mutual trust and security never develops. When this ensues, you enter a constant state of what is called *attachment distress*.

Attachment and the Distress of Disconnection

Returning to our discussions of attachment, recall what happens when you reach for comfort or reassurance and do not receive it. You return to a feeling state similar to that of the upset child who does not obtain the comfort he or she desires. You may feel a mix of emotions: fear, sadness, anguish, even panic. These feelings make you try harder to get reassurance. This may take the form of poking, pushing, seeking, clinging, nagging, or demanding behaviors. When you still do not find the sense of security you are looking for, an attachment panic, or distress, sets in. This may lead to despair and desperation. If your attempt at connection goes unrequited, you will linger in a state of despair or you will detach and go numb. Finally, the despair or detachment may ultimately motivate you to leave this circumstance and move on. Getting to this point comes at a high emotional cost, so I encourage exiting this situation sooner rather than later.

Here's what attachment distress looked like in Zoey's relationship with Andrew. Zoey often felt ignored, unappreciated, and let down by Andrew. The more emotionally unavailable he became, the harder she would try to fix the relationship. However, Zoey was turning into someone she barely recognized in the mirror. Before meeting Andrew, she had done pretty well. But that changed when she met him. He had a wicked sense of humor and was exactly her type. She fell head over heels for him, but Andrew wasn't as serious about the relationship as Zoey was. He never directly communicated this to her, but he would pull away, sometimes "forget" to call her back, make plans with friends without checking with her, and derail any conversations about their relationship.

During one of Zoey's attempts at a conversation about the relationship, Andrew walked out of the living room and into the bedroom and locked the door. Zoey banged on the door, cried, and pleaded with him to keep talking. When she realized it was going nowhere, she gave up, sat back down on the couch, and cried all alone. At times like this, the distress of disconnection first gave way to panic, and then helplessness set in. Sometimes, it would get resolved later when Andrew decided to revisit the discussion, but other times he refused to talk about the topic further. Repeated cycles of fighting like this took a heavy toll on Zoey but seemed not to faze Andrew. This left her in a constant state of ambivalence about whether to stay with him or leave the relationship.

The success of the second phase of love is highly contingent upon you and your partner having both *trust* and *attunement* — two concepts that I discuss further in chapter 11. But let's briefly look at them now. Trust in a relationship is about knowing and feeling that a partner is reliable, so that you feel safe and secure with him on both a physical and an emotional level. The partner's intentions for the relationship are transparent and forthcoming. Attunement involves the emotional connection you have with a partner. The core of *attunement* contains the word *tune* for a good reason. With positive attunement, you find it relatively easy to tune in to yourself and your partner's world so you both may respond appropriately to each other's cues, emotional state, and emotional needs. When misattunement occurs, there is also a clear pathway to reattune and repair the relationship. When this does not readily happen, attachment distress is the result.

Protest Behavior

When you reach to connect with your partner, you're doing what the prominent relationship researcher Dr. John Gottman calls a "bid for connection." Your partner has a choice in how to respond. Bids like this can range from small and subtle to large and clear. He can turn toward you, and the connection can occur, or he can choose to turn away, and the connection doesn't happen. Continually turning away from a partner erodes the bond, causing distress and disconnection in the relationship. It may also trigger protest behaviors in you.

Here are some examples of Nadine's more subtle bids for connection with Eric. She would send him funny jokes during the day by text. When they were together, she would try to discuss Eric's favorite music. Nadine would also ask if he could call her to say good night in the evenings. Eric had a choice. He could respond in kind, acknowledging her efforts and longings (turning toward), or he could disregard her efforts and longings (turn away). The way each responds to the other creates the possibility for connection if an exchange goes well or disconnection if it goes poorly.

Common protest behaviors that occur when bids for connection go unheeded include the following:

- Excessively trying to make contact: calling, texting, or emailing multiple times; dropping by unannounced; lurking on social media; asking friends to spy
- Manipulating: pretending you don't care, acting vengeful, ignoring, lying, acting helpless, crying, making him jealous
- Withdrawing: getting back by ignoring, walking away, numbing out, obsessing over the situation, staying unproductive
- Scorekeeping: playing games, purposely not responding, or waiting the same amount of time that your partner waited to reply
- Showing hostility: being belligerent or contemptuous, having tantrums or outbursts
- Giving ultimatums or making empty threats
- Hooking up with someone else or telling him you will

Doing any of these behaviors is understandable when your attachment alarms are going off. However, they are ineffective. You will unwittingly become an active participant in the dance of disconnection.

Sex, Love, and Intimacy

Both men and women sometimes confuse sex for love and/ or intimacy. Women, however, often find themselves settling for sex when they are really seeking intimacy. This can make for a dissatisfying and confusing experience with a romantic partner, so it's important to clear up this issue. You can have sex with someone you do not love. You can have sex for recreation, to relieve stress, or for any other reason you wish to have it. Sex, however, is also an expression of love or a way in which we build intimacy with another person. Intimacy involves feeling close and connected with another. There are many ways to build intimacy, such as communicating with each other, engaging in caring behaviors, and being affectionate, as well as having sex. For many, having sex when you are not sure there is love can be a hollow and unfulfilling act.

Sex can also ignite the neurochemicals and neurotransmitters involved in the feeling of love. Hence, it may add to your confusion, leading you to call the feeling love when, really, you are just having sex. Waiting longer to have sex for the first time with someone will help you slow down to see if the relationship has real potential and whether the development of shared trust and security is sustainable. This is even more crucial for women, who are wired a little differently in this area than men. Men more readily have sex with another person whether or not they have loving feelings for that person, and they feel less guilt or confusion afterward. Most women are not wired that same way, and therefore they are more susceptible to being hurt if they thought the sex was an expression of love but find that for him it was just for fun.

I know that there are exceptions to the rule, so perhaps some guidelines will help you better navigate the sex-and-intimacy topic. It is advised that you don't have sex unless you are able to have a conversation about sex first. The conversation should clarify what it means to each of you and what your expectations are for your relationship. The key is that you both are in *agreement* regarding what the sex is about. If you both want to relieve stress, fine, but if one of you wants to relieve stress and the other is looking to deepen the romantic connection, you have a problem. This might seem unromantic, but if you want to avoid hurt and embarrassment, you need to have this talk.

Unfortunately, Carla made the mistake of having sex without first talking about it, numerous times. She thought having sex with men would make them fall in love with her. She even seduced a man who had broken up with her to be with another woman. She thought she could win him back this way, but it didn't work. With the men she really liked, Carla never talked about the relationship and where things were headed. She worried that the discussion would be too awkward and might even scare the guy off. Carla eventually had an epiphany about her sexual behavior with these men: they usually left her anyway, most of their time together was spent in bed, they had little to talk about when out of bed, she felt alone when apart from them, and she had interpreted their sexual interest in her as a validation of her worth. She was confusing sex and intimacy, and it was affecting her greatly.

Love and Commitment

The final phase of love, the one you may be looking to achieve, is commitment. Committing without successfully going through the first two phases of love is a terrible idea. Some people have the notion that committing, or getting married, will cure the problems they are having in the earlier phases or the dating process. This is a dangerous fallacy that you should not buy into.

This phase of love is about being loyal to one another, continuing to nurture your ongoing love, and making a promise to do this forever. It will flourish only if you both have done an adequate job of building it earlier in your relationship. This commitment may take the form of marriage, or it may not.

Whether or not the "piece of paper" has meaning for you both is a personal choice. *What matters most is that you both want the same things for your relationship and each other at the same time.*

Some Final Thoughts about Love

The Beatles song "All You Need Is Love" is a popular song with a great tune. But I'm sorry to say that it is based on a myth that you should not believe either. You should not use the term *love* to describe your feelings for another unless you can also say you feel safe, secure, and at peace with the other person. If you cannot, it is not love; likely your attachment system is activated instead.

If you have gotten this far in the chapter, I'm certain it's clear why you need more than love to have a thriving relationship. The *feeling* of love, or simply using the word *love*, is unquestionably not enough to produce trust, security, attunement, and so on. You need loving feelings along with all the other ingredients and skills to be both a good partner and the right partner.

One other popular belief is that there is a one-and-only soul mate for you. When you are enthralled in the limerence and lust phase of love, it is natural to think that you must have found your soul mate. It may be confusing to hear that this person is not your soul mate, and that, in fact, you may have these feelings for the wrong person! The truth is that there are many different people on the planet that you could fall in love with. You just won't meet all of them, so you won't have the opportunity. Understanding this can go a long way in helping you stay hopeful. If you are in love with someone who is not loving you back in the way you want to be loved, I promise there is a better match out there for you.

CHAPTER SEVEN

WHEN YOU NEED TO BREAK UP (AND HOW TO DO IT)

B reaking up with someone you have strong feelings for, perhaps even "love," is no easy task. By now, hopefully, you know whether you are in an unhealthy dynamic in your current relationship and whether you have an emotionally unavailable partner (or potential partner). If your reasonable attempts to find a secure connection go unheeded, I strongly advise you to consider breaking up with this person.

If you are involved with a married man, you absolutely must break up, because this is a sure dead end for you. However, the last thing you *want* to do is break up with this person. What you really desire is to have this person love you back and treat you the way you treat him. Breaking things off with someone you don't wish to have a relationship with is tough enough; breaking things off with someone you do care about is substantially more difficult. However, if you want to find unequivocal love, you must take serious action by dissolving this relationship and making a clear plan to move forward.

Reasons to Break Up

First and foremost, *you are allowed to break up with anyone for any reason.* You do not need special permission. I have heard many people say they avoided breaking off a relationship because they feared being lonely or wanted to avoid hurting someone. These are perhaps the worst reasons to *not* break up. Moreover, you should be clear about the reasons you want to split up, and you should understand that those reasons are okay. There is no need to feel guilty for doing what is best for you, your life, and your future.

Here are some reasons why breaking off your current relationship is a smart decision:

- **You are unhappy or distressed and attribute this emotional state to the relationship.** If you are in a constant state of sadness and despair, you should listen to these feelings. Some people describe feeling lonelier in a disconnected relationship than when they are truly alone. Another common feeling that people mention is that they are on a perpetual roller coaster when it comes to the relationship. Emotions like these, along with your gut feelings, should guide your decision about whether to end it. Make it about you and your thoughts and feelings, not about someone else's.

- **The bad outweighs the good.** This part can trip you up. There are, for sure, good times. And you will cling to these good times as both a reminder and evidence of his love and care. However, this isn't sensible. Many people make this erroneous justification in their minds. The bad should be minimal and should only be "normal bad." Examples of "normal bad" include arguing over what movie to see, the shoes that were left out to trip on, or whose turn it is to take out the dog. Not abuse bad. Not serial cheating bad. Not married to someone else bad. And certainly not emotionally unavailable bad!

- **You have lost trust.** If you have lost trust, your relationship has developed a cracked foundation. The foundation can be repaired with intentional effort on the part of the person who betrayed your trust. Without this, a cloud of suspicion will hang over the relationship and will not disperse.

  Losing trust can happen when you experience betrayal, such as cheating. It can also occur when you repeatedly experience your partner as unavailable emotionally. When your partner turns away from the relationship instead of toward you to meet his needs, distrust and doubt will develop. And mistrust will develop if he meets your needs inconsistently or not at all. Bad behavior may not be as obvious as cheating; that's why it's imperative to understand that not trusting your partner on any emotional level is significant. In attachment language, this is when the answer to the question "Will you be there for me?" is likely a "no."

- **It's hard to envision a future.** Wanting a future with this person and being able to envision a future with him are two separate concerns. If you close your eyes and cannot visualize a clear path to marital bliss, growing old together, or making some form of commitment, this is problematic. You might not be sure how this will look because of your current state of affairs. If your life together has been rocky, the future probably looks blurry. The past holds critical clues to the future, because you will get more of the same, or worse — worse because, ironically, many bad behaviors become exacerbated or more difficult to tolerate the longer you are together (not the other way around).

It may also be a challenge to imagine a future if your family dislikes your partner. It might be the case that your family is messed up and your partner is healthy. But this describes only a minority of situations. If those who care about you — your family or friends — have a strong dislike for your partner, you should give this serious consideration. They can see things you may be blind to. Take time to think about whether your partner will easily integrate into and be accepted by your circle of friends and family.

Eileen struggled with all the above reasons to break up with Frank. There were very passionate and fun times, but there were seriously tumultuous times. She described the relationship as a roller coaster, and the bad outweighed the good. The difficulties chipped away at the emotional trust. She did not know if the problem was her, him, or them together. Simply trying to figure out what had gone wrong so she could fix things between them exhausted her. When she thought about the future, she felt physically ill. She could not picture Frank as her life partner or the father of her children! She made the brave decision to break up. Frank took it so poorly that she ended up having to block him from her phone and social media. Afterward, Eileen went through a tough period and even missed Frank, but she knew deep down it was the right decision.

What to Say and Do

There is never a perfect time to break up with someone you love, but certain circumstances make it more amicable. I do not recommend ghosting someone, as tempting as that might be. You can and should bring empathy and integrity to the process and apply the golden rule.

After you have made the decision to end the relationship, avoid doing it during certain circumstances. You should not have the breakup conversation if your partner is midcrisis — for example, if he has just experienced a death in the family or was diagnosed with an illness. Don't derail your plan indefinitely, but let some time pass before having the talk.

Do not break up with someone in the middle of a fight, either, as appealing as this may seem to be. I have heard of people who purposely wait for a conflict to do it, and that's a poor strategy. It does take more courage to wait until a calmer moment, but doing so will bring integrity to the process. It will be better for you, both now and in the future, to do it the right way, even though this person may not deserve it.

You may have the breakup conversation in public, but not in earshot of others. Finally, do not break up by text, email, or phone; you should have the conversation face-to-face. A few exceptions to this rule exist: you are long-distance, you are fearful of the reaction, or you have had only a few dates.

Don't let the breakup discussion come out of left field. You should prepare your partner for the conversation beforehand by making sure you have the time and place to do it. Begin the conversation gently by saying, "I would like to talk to you about something," or something similar. If you need to send a text or email in advance to secure the time and place, that is fine. And it is acceptable to indicate that you need to have a serious conversation.

There is no need to criticize or blame your partner when you are breaking up. Even though you probably have a laundry list of complaints, airing them will not be beneficial at this point. It will only make him defensive. Be honest but never harsh. How honest to be is a tough call. I advise making only general comments, unless you have incompatible interests or agendas. For example, it's fine to say, "I want kids and you don't," or "I'm a homebody, and you love to go out all the time." If you are unsure how much to say, stick to the generalities, especially if the primary reason is emotional unavailability.

Make the reasons more about you, and use a lot of "I" statements. In sticking with generalities, you can make statements like these:

- "I am not certain I see a future with us."
- "I need someone I feel I am more on the same page with."
- "I don't feel like we are compatible."
- "It's not going to work for me to wait around any longer for you to commit to me."

You do not have to give an ultimatum. Again, you are making it about your needs, your future, your desires, and your boundaries. If the person pushes for further explanations or tries to argue, stand firm and repeat the same statements.

If the relationship has been abusive in any way, be very brief and matter-of-fact. Do not be excessively apologetic. This can be mistaken for ambivalence or leave you open to manipulation. If the person counters with anger, pushback, or escalation, immediately disengage — walk out or hang up the phone and block him.

Dealing with Manipulation

When you try to break things off, you may be faced with manipulations that make you question or feel bad about your personal decision. Manipulators exploit your weaknesses. They know just what to say to make you feel bad and change your mind to get what they want. To combat manipulation, you must be unmoved by their arguments. You must be assertive and firm when you talk. Do not overexplain or overapologize. Draw the line where you want to draw it regarding any further communication on the topic of breaking up.

Melanie did not clearly see at first that her boyfriend, Guy, was being manipulative when she tried to break up with him. She was very unhappy in the relationship and knew she should move on. She attempted to break up with him three times before being able to do so for good. Each time was worse than the last, and she let six months go by between attempts.

When Melanie initially tried to have this difficult conversation, she was honest and sensitive. She could not see a future with Guy and did not wish to waste any more time with him. When she told him, he broke down in tears. And when she tried to console him, his sadness quickly turned to anger. He accused her of lying to him and leading him on. He even threw at her the fact that they had slept together the previous week, asking, "How could you do that when you probably knew then that you were going to leave me?" Melanie felt terribly guilty and couldn't bear to hear more. She started to believe that she was wrong for doing this to Guy. She relented, and after a short period of calm when they resumed the relationship, she started to feel Guy was punishing her. He would slip in sarcastic remarks whenever he could about her attempt to break up. When she reached her breaking point, she tried again to end the relationship with Guy and was again unsuccessful. This time, Guy went ballistic over the fact that Melanie was doing this "right before Christmas," telling her how embarrassed he would be in front of his family members who were coming to town for the holidays. Melanie stood her ground and walked out. But a few days later, Guy called her, weeping. He apologized, proclaimed how much he loved her, and told her that he had bought her the most amazing gift for the holidays. He said he would get help for all the things he was doing wrong.

When Melanie broke up with Guy for the third and final time, it was a disaster. When he realized this time it was final, after more manipulation attempts had failed, he upped the ante. He posted publicly on social media about the breakup and how heartbroken he was. He came by her apartment and left on her doorstep a pile made up of every gift she had given him and every love note she had written him. He also started to befriend some of her friends to keep tabs on her life. Needless to say, Guy was a major manipulator who made it excruciatingly difficult for Melanie to break up. She was upset at herself for not succeeding the first time, because she'd known in her gut and in her heart that this was what she needed to do.

No Easy Way

There's no easy way to break up. I wish there were. I wish there were something between staying and going, but there isn't. Breaking up is a leap into the unknown, at least at first. You should know that you may never get back together or even see this person again. But going back and forth will cause damage to the relationship that may be permanent.

Breaking up is a highly emotional process, and trying to be friends after a breakup is unrealistic and unwise. It will hinder your healing process. It may also create roadblocks for you when you try to meet someone new. Sometimes people say, "Can we be friends?" to reduce the pain of loss. You should not suggest it, and if your partner does, firmly say no.

If you don't see each other regularly at work or school, it will be easier for you to avoid contact. But if you do see this person regularly, you may want to change your schedule, job, or other circumstances so you do not see him. Do not follow him on social media or respond to any attempts at communication. Interacting with him will impede the breakup process and your emotional healing.

Sudden Availability

Someone emotionally unavailable may suddenly become extremely available once the two of you break up. This is a common and insincere reaction. The tables have turned, and now you are being pursued as you always wanted. You may hear all sorts of promises of change. This is alluring, but don't fall for it. It is temporary, and an attempt to get you back. Your relationship's status quo will be reinstated soon after you go back. This is still part of the same behavior and personality traits that are making you miserable. It is nothing new or different.

Let's take a look at how Jenny handled splitting up with Dave. She had several reasons to break up with him. She was dissatisfied with the relationship overall and never seemed to feel at ease. He was inconsistent and unreliable, often leaving her feeling off-balance with him. She believed this man was bringing out the worst in her, because she found herself acting in ways she never had before, such as by constantly attempting to find ways to get his attention. By communicating clearly and directly, she tried in a mature manner to get him to understand what was going on for her. But she would leave their conversations feeling dismissed. When she tried to imagine a future with Dave, she had trouble. She did not feel secure and confident in him or the relationship.

When Jenny decided to break up with Dave, she wanted to do it smartly and maturely. First, she asked to meet with him. At their meeting, she calmly let him know she was unhappy, that she could not see a future for them, and, furthermore, that she was ending the relationship. She was flabbergasted by how hurt he was and that he said she had blindsided him. He tearfully begged her not to leave and promised to be a better boyfriend. Suddenly she felt as if cement blocks were attached to her feet, and that she couldn't walk away. All she wanted to do was stay and console him. She felt guilty for breaking up with him but, deep down, knew she could not be responsible for his reaction. She briefly stated that she was sorry for causing him pain but was determined to carry out her breakup plans.

Jenny soon shifted her focus to how she had been feeling the past four months — miserable. She also reflected upon how she had tried discussing her dissatisfaction on several occasions, and that nothing had ever changed. She finally found the strength to walk away from the conversation and him, saying her decision was final and that she wanted him to respect it. He asked to stay friends, but she replied that it was not a good idea right now. Right after leaving, she called her best friend, Sandy, who validated her decision to break up. After all, Sandy had seen her best friend unhappy and anxious for months because of Dave.

Seek Support

One of the toughest times for you will be right after you break up. It is helpful to spend as much time as possible with supportive friends and family after a split. Don't be bashful about reaching out to others and talking about what's going on. A therapist can also help you immensely as you process and reflect upon what has happened and can keep you focused on the future. Alone time is good as well, but you may be more at risk of going back to the relationship if you spend too much time alone.

At this point it will be helpful to make a plan for coping with the complicated and painful feelings that come with a breakup. The painful feelings make it easy to slide back into the relationship, repeatedly. Above all, you will want to learn how to choose wisely so that you can enjoy the secure, loving, and trusting relationship you and a partner are both worthy of and entitled to.

CHAPTER EIGHT

HOW YOUR EMOTIONS TELL YOU WHAT YOU NEED

Our emotions are our internal subjective experience of the world and our interactions with other people. These emotions are the result of our perceptions of situations, along with the resulting physiological responses within our bodies. We give a name to an emotion, such as anger, sadness, or joy, based on our interpretation of the cue (the situation or person) that set it off, and on our interpretation of our bodily sensations. Many things influence our experience and expression of emotion: our past experiences, what we have been taught, our culture, socialization, and so on. The patterns you tend to find yourself in with romantic partners (and with friends and family) mirror your internal emotional struggles. Therefore, given their subjectivity, emotions should not be viewed as right or wrong or good or bad. It is most helpful to view emotions as instrumental in motivating us to act and respond. What you do with the emotions, the choice you make about how to respond, is what we wish to change (not the emotion itself). This may sound surprising, but emotions are also the key to effectively communicating within a relationship.

Understanding Emotion

Having a basic understanding of emotions can be helpful if you are trying to change or manage your feelings and behavior. Emotions, shaped over time through evolution, have allowed you to navigate and adjust to your environment. Take fear, for instance. Feeling fear told us that there was a danger in the environment (such as the imminent possibility of being chased by a lion) so that our brains and bodies could spring into action and we could run fast to safety. As you can surmise, a person who could experience fear was more likely to survive than one who could not. Negative emotions, such as fear or disgust, dissuade us from harmful or damaging behavior. Similarly, positive emotions, such as happiness, motivate us to engage in potentially productive behaviors. Understanding emotion is essential to our ability to survive, thrive, and generally make good decisions.

Psychology theorists tend to agree that six basic emotions exist, and that they are experienced in all cultures. These are happiness, sadness, surprise, anger, fear, and disgust. More recently, researchers have added contempt, shame, love, pride, and anxiety. These emotions are universal, yet how and when they are expressed differs quite a bit depending on cultural norms. Your emotions affect the way others see and treat you. They also influence your personal sense of well-being.

The limbic system of the brain is the location for emotion,

memory, behavior, and motivation. This part of our brain is instrumental in helping us survive by scanning the environment for danger signs. Within the limbic system is the amygdala, which is responsible for "fear conditioning" — in other words, where we learn to fear something. You were not born fearing a parent, for example, but may have learned to do so if he or she was abusive. This ultimately leads to a lot of confusion about loving and caring relationships. The brain is highly complex, and we won't spend a lot of time on it. Suffice it to say that you need to know that you are always scanning for danger (or safety). This ability helps you survive and get through life. But if your danger cues are confused, your scanning reflex may be in overdrive.

A major component of emotion involves our physiological, or bodily, sensations. You experience many different bodily sensations and physical changes, depending on the emotion you are feeling. At its core, having a gut response, or almost automatic physical response, is called *visceral*, whereas *somatic* sensations arise from the mind, or intellect. Examples of physiological sensations are things like sweating, tension, heart racing, chest tightness, flushed face, and so on. There is a wide range, and what a person experiences may vary, depending on the feeling itself and on the individual. Learning to sense and identify a physical sensation can often clue you in to what you are feeling, especially if you have trouble recognizing and naming your feelings.

Many people erroneously believe our emotional experiences and reactions are beyond our control. A part of your emotional reaction is controlled by your own body's physiology and genetic predispositions. Other parts involve both the context and the people around you. *Emotional contagion*, or being affected by others' emotional experiences, is also a very real phenomenon. Regardless of influences, you have much more power over your emotional response than you realize.

Emotions and Attachment

Your early (FOO) attachment history affects your perception and expression of emotion. Our earliest emotions as infants involve the desire for connection and to be taken care of and responded to when hungry, hurt, or in need of physical contact and attention. Not all parents or caretakers easily pick up cues or react to them. They may lack the emotional attunement to do so, or they have struggled with their own personal emotional shortcomings. Like attachment, your emotional development is a multifaceted process that begins at birth and continues into adulthood.

Secure attachment fosters an overall positive view and expression of both negative and positive emotions. A secure child receives a clear and consistent message that emotional expression will be responded to in a meaningful and appropriate way, and that he or she can express anger or jealousy and not be treated harshly or rejected for the expression. When a child's feelings are regularly ignored, the child stops readily communicating them because "no one will respond anyway," which can lead to an avoidant attachment. Furthermore, when a child is given the negative message that he or she is "needy" for expressing emotional needs, those needs get cranked down or turned off. Or the child can become overwhelmed by having to cope with feelings on his or her own. When a child's emotional expression is misunderstood, met with anger, or shamed, this can lead to the development of insecure attachment. The child's ability to communicate attachment-related feelings and needs is *disavowed*.

Think about how emotions were dealt with in your family of origin. Here are several questions to help you get a sense of your early experiences related to emotion:

- What messages did you get when you expressed anger, hurt, shame, fear, and so on?
- Were there certain feelings you were not allowed to express or share?
- Did you have someone there to help you make sense of negative things that may have happened to you?
- Did you have someone there to comfort you when you had emotional distress?
- When you expressed emotional needs, such as the need for comfort, reassurance, attention, and affection, was it safe to do so?
- Were the responses appropriate and consistent?
- Did your parents express emotion, caring, and love clearly and effectively? If not, why do you think this happened?
- What do you know about your parents' FOO history that may have influenced their ability to respond to you adequately?

Take some time to reflect on these questions. Allow yourself to be curious about the emotional influences during your life. If it is helpful, you may use a journal to write down what comes to mind. It is okay to jot down your thoughts as you reflect upon these questions over time.

Let's look at the instance of little Joey. Joey's father was aloof and distant, and he showed his son little physical affection. He also criticized Joey if he ever cried, even if he got physically hurt. His mother was more loving and responded much more kindly to his expression of pain or fear. She heaped on the compassion, empathy, and care. Sometimes she would rescue him from his father's rants. The parents' opposite ways of dealing with Joey's expression of needs and emotions were confusing to him. He learned that he could cry only to his mother, and that when his father was around he had to act tough and show little emotion. He began to depend excessively on his mother, often clinging to her. This would further enrage his father, who would sometimes call him a "big baby" or a "wuss."

As an adult, Joey struggled a lot with relationships. His girlfriend thought he was a "mama's boy." Even as an adult, he would talk to his mom daily. He called her for advice and to vent about his relationships, and he would go home for her home-cooked meals. He also expected his girlfriends to take care of him seemingly all the time, getting sullen and withdrawn when it didn't happen. He had difficulty being independent and reaching out to age-appropriate peers or girlfriends to get his needs met. Inside, he thought of himself as incapable and weak. Joey had internalized his early experiences with mixed emotional messages in his FOO, creating an insecure attachment style in adulthood. His response to his emotional needs (for comfort and reassurance) had become unhealthy in his adult romantic relationships.

Repetitive patterns in our experiences with emotion and the expression of emotional needs create an inner template, or mental representation, of our world, ourselves, and others. From this template, also called a *working model*, we develop beliefs and expectations about how we will be treated.

Sometimes we create a repressed, shameful, negative self-image. We may think we are unlovable, unworthy, or undeserving. This self-image gives rise to feelings of rejection, abandonment, shame, and fear. You believe that you are treated badly because you *are* bad. The quality of attachment, or the lack of attachment, is a long-lasting and enduring element embedded in your personality, perceptions, and experience of emotion.

Emotion Awareness

Knowing what you feel and why is called emotional awareness. This helps you know what you need or want and what you don't need or want in life and from others. Being emotionally aware helps you choose and create better relationships. This is because emotional awareness can help you identify and communicate about your feelings in a clear way. You will be more effective at managing conflict, resolving problems, strategizing how to get your needs met, and moving past difficult feelings. Being conscious of your emotions and putting your emotions into words (emotional fluency) comes more naturally to some, based on their history and experiences. Emotional awareness and fluency can also be practiced and developed. Doing so builds *emotional intelligence*, a skill that helps you succeed in life, work, and relationships. I elaborate on the concept of emotional intelligence in chapter 11, on healthy relationships.

Emotions can be transient, and we can feel various emotions throughout the day. But if an emotion lingers for a while, it becomes a "mood." If you are in a heartbroken state, you are likely in a down mood that seems to be a dark cloud following you everywhere. You may fall into a clinical depression requiring therapeutic intervention and medication. Your emotions may range anywhere from mild to severe. The intensity varies depending on the situation. Emotions are not good or bad — but there are good and bad ways of handling them. Awareness and understanding of emotions create a foundation to build effective and healthy ways to manage them.

Emotions usually aren't pure. You can feel a mix of emotions, like sadness and hurt. There is strong evidence that emotion is the first response to experience, even if you are not aware of what you are feeling at first. This is contrary to some previous assertions that perceptions and thoughts come first, before the feeling. Our emotional experience in reaction to something frequently has a "surface" part as well as a "deeper" part. In other words, the surface emotion is a reactive or defensive emotion expressed outwardly, such as anger. But the inner, deeper, underlying emotion might be hurt or shame. The deeper emotion is what comes up immediately in response to a situation or event. Therefore, the surface emotion can send an inaccurate signal to others. Unsuccessful attempts to be aware of, soothe, and clearly communicate the deeper, more vulnerable emotions is what becomes problematic in your personal relationships. For instance, if you are sad but express anger, it may push someone away. But if you are sad and are able to vulnerably communicate this in a clear and heartfelt way, it may draw the other person toward you. This is important, because sending clear messages about your feelings and needs helps those around you understand and help you in your moments of distress.

The Flow of Emotion

Here is what unfolds, quite rapidly, when you are triggered by someone or something. It is laid out here as a flowchart, but perhaps a chart with a circular pattern would be more fitting, because after the initial trigger, the rest of the "flow" moves rather synergistically. For instance, your perceptions and actions may trigger more emotion and bodily arousal and so on.

Situation/Trigger
(What happened to you?)

Quick Assessment
(Is this situation or trigger safe or dangerous?)

Bodily Arousal
(How your body reacts.)

Perceptions/Thoughts
(What does this situation or trigger mean?
What do you tell yourself?)

Feelings
(What do you feel? What are your defensive
feelings and deeper feelings?)

Behavior/Reaction
(What do you do? What do you really need?)

Here's an example of Lynn's flow of emotion:

Situation/Trigger: Boyfriend ignores my texts and calls.

⬇

Quick Assessment: I'm being abandoned once again.

⬇

Bodily Arousal: Heart racing, tension in my body.

⬇

Perceptions/Thoughts: I'm unlovable and unimportant.

⬇

Feelings: Defensive = anger; deeper = scared and hurt.

⬇

Behavior/Reaction: Send several nasty texts to him, threaten to break up; what I need: I really wish he would make me feel like a priority and reassure me more.

What would Lynn do instead if she were to practice better emotional awareness and emotional management? She would tune in to her deeper emotion, acknowledge it, and think about what triggered her. She reflects upon how neglectful her parents were. This is quite painful for her. It has become her personal "danger signal." When she senses she is ignored, her anger usually flares up very quickly.

I emphasize that, given her history and experiences, her reaction is not abnormal. Being the "squeaky wheel" as a child may have helped get her parents to pay attention to her. But now, in her adult life, it works rather poorly. When slowing down her reaction, she can think more astutely about what is happening in these moments and what to do. The next time, instead of sending a nasty text in anger, she sends a text to her boyfriend that says, "Please call me at your convenience today. I have something important to tell you." When her boyfriend finally calls several hours later, she tells him, "I was hurt that you took an entire day to get back to me. When you ignore me like that, I wonder how important I really am to you or whether you care about us." If her boyfriend responds lovingly — for example, by apologizing and giving her a hug — the misattunement is repaired. If he calls her "needy" or "paranoid" or has some other undesirable reaction, it should tell her that this guy does not want to respond, or is incapable of responding, to her emotional needs. At this point, Lynn has a choice when she decides what she wants to do about the relationship. If she chooses to break it off, she will need to effectively manage her emotions in order to get through this stressful event.

Figuring Out Your Flow of Emotion

Now, it's time to try and figure out your own flow of emotion. You can think about your current relationship, your last relationship, or how you generally feel, act, and respond in relationships. You may use an app or journal to record your responses. Answer the following questions:

- What are typical situations that trigger you?
  Examples: not responding to my complaints, ignoring me, blowing off plans, not being able to talk about "us," making me the bad guy / crazy one / needy one for asking for what I need, teasing me, putting me down, paying more attention to something other than

me, drinking too much, shutting me out, acting like we're not together.

- What is your quick assessment of the perceived danger that comes from these situations?
  Examples: abandonment, disconnection, instability, a lack of safety, rejection.
- What do you sense in your body?
  Examples: racing heart, dry mouth, spinning head, desire to flee, frozen sensation, knot in the stomach, chest tightness, difficulty breathing, faintness, weakness, tearfulness.
- What do you say to yourself when this happens (based on FOO experiences)?
  Examples: I'm being abandoned/hurt/shunned, I'm not lovable, I'm not worthy, I'm not important, I'm always the one doing all the work, I'm alone, I'm not cared about.
- How do you cope with or defend against this distress?
  Examples: yell, poke, criticize, demand, try harder, seduce, walk away, get self-destructive, get revenge, insult, act out, withdraw, drink, check out.
- What feeling(s) do you show?
  Examples: anger, sadness, rage, frustration, hurt, jealousy, confusion.
- What do you really feel deep down?
  Examples: sadness, hurt, pain, rejection, loneliness, isolation.
- What do you hope will happen?
  Examples: He will realize what he is doing, he will make changes, he will respond to me, he will love me back, he will make it all okay.
- What do you really need?

Examples: someone responsive to my feelings, an equal partner, mutual appreciation, someone who understands me, someone who puts me first, someone who shows empathy.

Learning about your attachment style and early FOO experiences helps you understand how you came to your unique perception of social threats, the way you interact with others, and the manner in which you process emotions. These elements work in cooperation to play a significant part in whether a romantic relationship flourishes or fails. This knowledge will prevent your emotions from both hijacking your thoughts and responding problematically. Your emotions can be used to effectively solve interpersonal problems and respond strategically when you are triggered. Once you recognize the "traps" inherent in an emotionally unavailable partner, you recognize how you get stuck and how to get yourself out. The next chapter can help you understand how to cope with difficult emotions if you decide to get out of a relationship with someone emotionally unavailable.

CHAPTER NINE

TOLERATING THE PAIN OF A BREAKUP IF YOU NEED TO WALK AWAY FOR GOOD

One of the most challenging times in life occurs after the breakup of a romantic relationship. It's a time of significant stress, to say the least. Often, it is the reason people decide to seek therapy, sometimes for the first time in their lives. It is dreadful when you are left heartbroken because someone you love has left you. It is also pretty awful when someone you love is not emotionally responsive and is playing games with your heart.

A breakup often triggers us to focus on what has transpired and replay it over and over. This process is termed *rumination*. You get stuck and continuously think about what happened, and why, from all angles. It is an attempt at problem-solving. However, not only does it not work, it also makes you feel worse and leads to more feelings of grief, anxiety, and depression. Rumination will continue to breathe life into your negative mood. If you are ruminating about something, you need to find something else to distract you. It doesn't matter what activity it is, but you must engage in something else to get your mind unstuck. Since it's impossible to will yourself to not think about it, you must replace the repetitive thoughts with different thoughts.

Limerence Gone Wrong

In chapter 6, I discussed the early stage of love, called limerence. In some of the psychological literature, the word *limerence* is also defined in a negative way, as the euphoric feelings of romantic love that some people continue to feel despite a lack of reciprocation. It's as if someone put the high of early love into a bowl, added some addiction and some obsessive-compulsive disorder, and stirred it all up. When someone does not reciprocate your feelings, yet your feelings intensify anyway, this is problematic.

These thoughts about and feelings for an unavailable partner may become pervasive and may even seem beyond your ability to control. The sense of uncertainty in the relationship is, paradoxically, a major driving force for your increasing romantic feelings. The constant search for signs that you are loved back gives way to mood fluctuations and, in extreme cases, may even diminish your ability to function. What's worse is if you do get some occasional positive signs in return. This will often prompt a feedback loop that makes you reciprocate in an even more intense way. The behavior of a person stuck in such a loop may become intense enough to be labeled obsessive-compulsive and addictive behavior.

Even when you're the "dumper" rather than the "dumpee," it is still tough. Therefore, learning to tolerate the pain and distress — and banish the rumination and self-defeating be-havior — that come with the end of a relationship will help you move forward confidently. It will also help prevent you from sliding down the slippery slope back into the relation-ship again. When your brain is hijacked and tells you to "just go back to him," you can find ways to respond differently and make a healthier choice. It is crucial for you to learn how to not only understand but also tolerate and manage your painful emotions.

An Integrative Approach to Managing Unpleasant Emotions

Ways of doing therapy have emerged from several psycho-logical theories about how emotion works. Using an inte-grative approach that combines several methods (drawing from methods such as cognitive-behavioral therapy, emotion-focused therapy, and mindfulness-based stress reduction), you can learn how to better manage and regulate your emotions during a difficult time such as heartbreak. The GET SMART acronym introduced in chapter 1 will help you formulate and remember your strategy to tolerate the pain of a breakup.

G — Goal Orientation

Becoming goal-oriented means focusing on what you wish to accomplish going forward. Create a specific goal for yourself for managing relationship-related distress. Make your goal state what you want, not what you don't want. Staying on track, even if you feel distressed, is critical. Not having any goals, or letting go of your goals, is more distressful. In fact, you will be happier in life if you continually create new goals for yourself. The value of goal creation may seem obvious, but it's surprising how many people are not able to clearly identify their goals. Chapter 10 discusses goal creation in depth.

E — Emotion Management

You've just learned a lot about emotions and the importance of having emotional awareness. Identifying your emotions, both the deeper underlying vulnerable emotion and the reactive or defensive emotions, is helpful when managing emotions. Developing tolerance, or the ability to regulate your emotions, is critical for moving past problems that can have you stuck. A troubled relationship and heartbreak are situations that people commonly get stuck in. There are three excellent strategies for developing emotional tolerance: *thought restructuring, self-soothing,* and *mindfulness practice.* These make up the next three letters of the acronym.

T — Thought Restructuring

Your thoughts are a powerful mechanism for producing an emotion. Psychologists long ago recognized this phenomenon and created some highly successful approaches to therapy using this concept (for example, cognitive-behavioral therapy and rational emotive therapy). Some thoughts are considered irrational or dysfunctional, and believing these thoughts can trigger negative feelings. Some thoughts are so pervasive they become the lens through which you view the world — a theme for you. For example, a negative thought might be "I am not capable of being assertive," and a negative theme is "I am not worthy." Thoughts and themes can be automatic, surfacing quickly, even unconsciously, in your mind. As you can imagine, living your life based on a negative theme is likely to make that belief come true. People tend to ruminate on such thoughts. Distorted thoughts, themes, and attitudes form a negative mind-set that consists of negative views of yourself, others, your world, your future, and ultimately, your feelings.

Cognitive-based therapies encourage us to challenge our negative thoughts, beliefs, and core themes by creating more balanced and realistic thoughts. The cognitive approach focuses fundamentally on changing thoughts only (and links thoughts to emotions slightly differently than explained in the previous chapter). The rationale for this approach is the idea that your feelings might be based on distorted thoughts at the get-go. Many of our distorted thoughts are presumed to become "automatic," popping up in our heads unconsciously. Making our thoughts positive is also worthwhile, but it is perfectly acceptable to keep them neutral instead. You can also pick apart the logic of negative thoughts and find evidence that the thoughts are not true, or figure out how the thoughts might be ineffective.

Here is the flow of negative cognitions:

Situation/Trigger
(What happened to you?)

**Perceptions / Negative Automatic Thoughts /
Dysfunctional Beliefs**
(What are you telling yourself?)

Feelings
(What do you feel?)

Behavior/Reaction
(What do you do?)

Reexamine Negative Automatic Thoughts / Dysfunctional Beliefs
(What is the evidence that the thoughts/beliefs are not true?
Are some of your thoughts irrational?
Can you come up with better, alternative thoughts instead?)

Feelings after Reexamining Thoughts/Beliefs
(Do you feel better after changing your thoughts and beliefs?)

Behavior/Reaction Based on Reexamined Thoughts/Beliefs
(What is a healthier alternative behavior?)

Here's an example of Lynn's cognitive flow:

Situation/Trigger: Sitting alone, dwelling on my breakup.

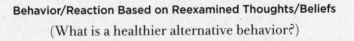

Perceptions / Negative Automatic Thoughts:
I will never find "the one,"
I'm unlovable and unworthy, men can't be trusted.
Dysfunctional Beliefs: I'm not worthy of love.

Feelings: Anger, hurt, sadness

Behavior/Reaction: Starting to cry.
I think maybe I should go back to him after all.

⬇

Reexamine Negative Automatic Thoughts:
It may not be about me at all; maybe it's about him,
and he isn't capable of being a good partner.
Many guys have had crushes on me, but I seem to
ignore the good ones. "Never" is a strong word;
I should change this to "might not find 'the one'" instead.

Reexamine Dysfunctional Beliefs:
Just because my dad didn't know how to love me does
not mean no one will love me! I expect to be treated
better and need to stop tolerating bad treatment.

⬇

Feelings after Reexamining Thoughts/Beliefs:
Less angry, hurt, and sad;
more motivated to move on without him.

⬇

Behavior/Reaction Based on Reexamined Thoughts/Beliefs:
I am going on a run with my favorite music on
my headphones, instead of just sitting here.
I will call my friends who are usually able to set me straight!

By examining her irrational and automatic thoughts and beliefs, Lynn found a way to alter them. This will help her stay realistic and rational about her relationships and her life. She is not going to react according to feelings that sprang from a faulty way of thinking. If Lynn changes a core negative belief, such as her perception that she is not lovable, to the belief that she is lovable, she will act in ways that bring healthy love into her life. When doing this thought-restructuring exercise yourself, you may not feel different initially, but over time you'll feel the positive effects of thinking differently.

You can also take cognitive strategies one step further. Do you remember all the hype around the concept of the "law of attraction" not too long ago? When I heard about this myself, I immediately thought it was another way to challenge negative thoughts and beliefs. Some of the ideas illustrated in the law of attraction are relevant in this area. A great takeaway is the underlying concept of changing negative thoughts to positive ones and developing positive expectations. It's not a bad idea to manifest your desire for love, a healthy relationship, or anything else you want out of life!

An additional cognitive strategy that may seem counter-intuitive, but is worth mentioning, has to do with *purposely* thinking negatively, particularly in respect to getting over heartbreak. In loss, our natural tendency is to idealize the person who is now gone. You can see how this can keep you stuck in pain over a former romantic partner. Therefore, purposely focusing on your ex's flaws and shortcomings, as well as reflecting on the negative aspects of your relationship, is helpful. I suggest taking it up a notch by writing a thorough list of these negatives and keeping it on your phone to refer to when you find yourself waxing poetic about your ex or the relationship.

S — Self-Soothing

Calming and comforting yourself are forms of self-soothing, a necessary skill when you're feeling overwhelmed or distressed. It is also helpful in various situations in life that you can't control. If you were not taught how to do this in your early years, you need to learn it now. You do not want to slide back into a bad relationship just because you have difficulty soothing yourself!

When you self-soothe, you turn inward in a caring way, instead of outward toward something harmful or unhealthy like alcohol or binge eating. You use your own internal resources to enable yourself to feel better. These resources usually involve your five senses: vision, hearing, smell, taste, and touch. The ability to self-soothe will come in handy when the pain and loneliness take hold after a breakup. It is a way to experience unpleasant emotions and let them eventually pass, without making them worse. Create a list of things that you experience through the five senses that you find appealing. Here is Lynn's list as an example.

- **Vision:** I love looking at impressionistic art. I will flip through my coffee-table book with those beautiful paintings. I also like to walk through the Japanese gardens near my home. I will head over there tomorrow.
- **Hearing:** I can't help but dance when I put on my favorite dance music. I will listen to my music every day for at least an hour. I'm sure I will get some exercise out of it, too!
- **Smell:** I can light my cinnamon-scented candles, since they are my favorite. I can also make cinnamon rolls, which will make my home smell nice all day.
- **Taste:** I will eat some cinnamon rolls for sure! I also like to drink herbal tea. I will see if a friend will go with me to my favorite tapas restaurant.
- **Touch:** I will take a warm bath and use a bath bomb. I will also warm up my towels in the dryer to use as soon as I get out of the bath, because I love that! I will spend more time petting and cuddling my dog.

You deserve such comforts, so don't ever think that you don't. It is not only acceptable but also necessary to comfort yourself. There is nothing wrong with it. Getting comfort from others is wonderful, but the reality is that this will not always be possible. Do not feel guilty seeking healthy, pleasurable activities that enliven your five senses.

M — Mindfulness

Mindfulness is about being fully engaged and aware of what is happening in the present moment without self-judgment. Mindful awareness can be cultivated in both the mind and the body. Mindfulness historically was spiritual, and it still can be. But today, people primarily use mindfulness to help cope with stress, negative feelings, chronic pain, mental health problems, and so on. Being mindfully aware will help you learn how to compassionately relate to the most important person in your life: YOU!

Mindfulness can be practiced in an entirely deliberate and formal manner, such as by doing meditation. Mindfulness meditation is a specific meditation practice that involves your body, posture, and breathing. The meditation focuses on awareness, inducing a relaxation response, and encourages a nonjudgmental, kind, and loving attitude toward oneself. This form of meditation is a tool to cultivate mindfulness in your everyday life, which is an excellent coping strategy. Anyone can learn this practice, but it may take formal instruction.

Mindfulness can also be practiced informally in everyday life activities. Both formal and informal practices have a lot to offer. Postbreakup, being mindful throughout the day can help you focus on tasks so that your mind does not continuously wander off into the realm of relationship pain. Mindfulness can also help you with the physiological stress reaction you are likely to be experiencing. The mind and body are interconnected. Calming your mind can help you harness the stress to respond more constructively. There is an excellent body of research that tells us that mindfulness is a powerful way to reduce stress, decrease a multitude of mental and physical symptoms, and improve one's quality of life.

You can definitely use mindfulness strategies when trying to get over the end of a relationship. Whereas cognitive strategies are used to alter thoughts, mindfulness encourages the acceptance of thoughts. Numbing your feelings is tempting. But why not allow yourself to feel, cry, grieve, and heal? Become aware of the array of emotions you are experiencing. Be compassionate and nonjudgmental toward yourself. Speak to yourself during this time as if you were talking to a child or a best friend.

Being rejected by one person does not give you much information about your lovability or your ability to find love in the future. And here's where your self-talk can help or hurt you. What you tell yourself about the breakup will have a significant impact on how you view your strengths and abilities. If this breakup teaches you that there is something you want to change about yourself, then, by all means, work on it. But be careful. Don't get so down on yourself that your nonjudgmental acceptance goes out the window.

Another mindful strategy is to avoid placing blame on anyone. Perhaps this relationship wasn't meant to be, and it isn't necessarily anyone's fault. Our minds tend to want to designate someone as culpable for what has transpired. Why not see change as inevitable, including in our romantic lives? Allow space for new possibilities. When one door closes, another one opens: it is a cliché but true. Being mindful during a breakup may seem foreign, but it doesn't have to be!

A — *Attachment Style*

Interwoven throughout this book are attachment concepts. Identifying your attachment style and how it has influenced your interpersonal behavior is critical. It will enable you to understand how you got into this relationship to begin with and how to get out and make better choices for yourself. Chapters 5 and 6 both delve into how your attachment style is formed early in life and the way in which it influences your current behavior in romantic relationships. In this section, I discuss more specifically how attachment affects relationship endings. You won't be surprised to know that your attachment system is activated at times of distress as well. A relationship breakup can be extremely distressing depending on how much time you've invested in it and how deeply in love you feel. Your attachment style can either help or hamper your ability to successfully transition out of the relationship and heal from what happened.

If you have a secure attachment style, you are most likely to have the healthiest reaction during a breakup and the transition to life without your partner. One reason is that those with a secure style tend to turn to healthier ways to cope. For example, they talk to close friends and family, exercise, and seek out enjoyable activities. They do not tend to get stuck in self-destructive patterns or turn to substances. They allow for a natural grief process and make efforts to comprehend what happened and why. Another critical piece of the picture is that those with a secure attachment style tend not to blame themselves or believe that they are unlovable. On the other hand, those with an insecure style are more likely to use unhealthy coping strategies, make attempts to get back into the relationship (even if it was unhealthy), and engage in behaviors that harm themselves and the partner who left them. Chapter 10 provides more details on how to accept the end of a relationship and move forward.

R — Reaching Out to Others

It is imperative to reach out to others for help, support, and comfort after a breakup. Help may come from friends, family, relatives, a support group, or a therapist. This is also a good time to find new friendships by engaging in various activities. An activity may be school- or work-related, a new hobby, involvement in a charity organization, or attendance at a place of worship.

Identify those in your support system who are good role models — healthy and resilient. Spend time with these people face-to-face. You may want to talk about the breakup, or you may just want company. Spend your time with those who value you, are a positive influence, and are likely to listen without judgment. If you do not have a strong support system, seeking out a therapist is a worthwhile endeavor. Do not try to deal with the breakup alone, because it will be much harder than if you engage your support system to help you through.

T — Transformed Behavior

Just because you are suffering, it does not mean you get a free pass to behave inappropriately. Acting vengeful, destructive, or impulsive will not help you get through your pain in the least. It is most critical that you resist "relapse" behavior as well. Going back and forth, in and out of the relationship, prolongs the pain and blocks the healing process. You must practice behaviors that are helpful, healthy, and positive.

It's beneficial, too, to put away (or delete) any photos you have of your former partner or of you as a couple. You should think deeply about deleting or suspending your social media accounts for a period of time as well. Social media can cause you unnecessary anguish when trying to get over a relationship. You should also remove or block your ex's number from your phone. Erasing traces of this relationship will help you move forward.

Do not stay in "victim" mode for too long. After a while, people will not want to hear endlessly about your ex. They will grow tired of whining and complaining. The sympathy and empathy you garner will be helpful until it reaches a saturation point. It may then contribute to a stuck mind-set. Make an effort not to speak your former partner's name or talk about all the awful things that were done to you. And don't go to places where you are likely to run into this person.

Do not, as tempting as it is, jump into another relationship. Allow yourself time to mourn the one you just ended. You will not be psychologically and emotionally available to someone else yet. You may be surprised to find that following these tips brings you much more quickly to the place where you are fully available to someone else.

Using the GET SMART strategy, you will be well on your way to getting though the ugly and painful part of a breakup. You don't have to let yourself be held hostage by an emotionally unavailable person! You have a lot more control over your feelings and behavior than you realize. Remember that your emotions are connected to your needs, and behind the most painful emotions is a longing. The longing is most often about reaching for and connecting with others, loving, and being loved.

Getting over the wrong person will open you up to the right person. The desire for a loving relationship will still be there. You do not have to remain stuck in a continuous grief process after one relationship ends.

CHAPTER TEN

MOVING FORWARD WITH CLARITY AND CONFIDENCE

Think about where you are right now in your life and relationships. If you are not satisfied, where do you wish to be instead? Are you able to imagine what life will look like when you get there? If you are thinking, "I want to be happy and in a loving relationship," then you want what nearly every human being wants! However, you have not explicitly described what this looks like or feels like to *you*. If you are currently evaluating your life and relationships because you got into a painful situation with an emotionally unavailable man, you need a clear picture of what you want your life to look like in the future. Do not meander through your life without a clear direction. You will need to know how to get where you want to go. This piece involves setting goals and making a road map to achieving them.

Setting Goals

Goal-setting is about identifying something you wish to accomplish for yourself. It can involve any aspect of your life: relationships, work, finances, health, and so on. You can work on changing a few things at once or focus on one primary goal at a time. Your goals should be grounded in your core value system. Goal-setting helps you stay proactive (not just reactive) about the aspects of your life you wish to change. Goal-setting should also be continual. When you achieve a goal, bask in the glory, and then set another one! People are happier and healthier when they continually have goals they are working toward and orient themselves toward growth.

One goal category should be "relationships," but you may have others as well. If you reflect on your core values, this will tell you where you should start. Core personal values are about your fundamental beliefs and the guiding principles you live by. These values dictate what is right or wrong for you and what is important to you. For example, in a relationship, your core values might include honesty, responsibility, industriousness, empathy, and commitment. You can design your relationship-related goals to encompass these values.

The goals you create most often relate to something you wish to achieve and are called *growth goals*. Maintaining a newly achieved goal is also part of the growth mind-set. But many people also develop goals to avoid certain outcomes, called *avoidance goals*. For example, if you are in a relationship with an emotionally unavailable man, your growth goal might be to end the relationship. If you are between relationships, your avoidance goal might be to stop yourself from getting into another unhealthy relationship. The components of goal-setting must be considered if you are to make your goals reachable and maintainable.

Goal Tracking: You will need a system to track your progress and stay accountable to yourself. If doing this on your own isn't your strong suit, find someone to assist you with this part. When we have another person to answer to, we are more inclined to stay on track. You can enlist a trusted confidant, coach, or therapist to help keep you on track.

It sounds simple, but using a calendar (either an "old school" calendar on paper or your phone's calendar) is always a good strategy. Every day, you can mark down the amount of progress you've made toward your goal. Several apps, too, are available specifically for goal tracking. Find one that works for your specific type of goal and lifestyle. You should have reminders every day that prompt you to keep moving toward your goals.

If you did not do well one day, do not get down on yourself or discouraged. The kind of changes you are looking to make are difficult, and backslides will happen. Do not tell yourself you can't do it or to forget about it. Ask yourself what happened that got you off track. What precipitated this backslide? Be curious and analytical instead of self-critical and negative.

Specific: Goals are detailed, precise, and explicit. They are not wishes, dreams, or fantasies. They are definitive and focused. You should have a clear image of how you, your life, and your relationships will look once you achieve the goal or goals you have set for yourself. You should be able to identify the who, what, why, where, and how of the goal. Goals should also be broken down into smaller, doable parts.

Measurable: You need a way to measure progress toward your goal. For some goals, progress is obvious. For example, if your goal is to lose ten pounds, the indicator on the scale stopping at a lower number shows that you're progressing toward your goal. But for life and relationship goals, the task of measuring progress is more difficult. If you are making a change in your dating or relationship patterns, you might measure the number of pages read in a self-help book, visits to a therapist, pages written in a journal, and daily uses of a mood-monitoring app.

Time frame: You should have an idea of the time frame in which you expect to reach either your goal or the smaller stepping-stones that your goal entails. Think about the point at which you believe you should reach, or make significant progress toward, your goal. You will want to think about what you can work on today and over the next week, month, or year. You should also be able to dedicate the time necessary to commit to the process of goal achievement.

Achievable: The goal must be realistic and attainable. Take under consideration everything that can help you reach your goal. This includes your internal and external resources, talents, skills, abilities, access to help and support, and so on. You already have within you many of the necessary skills and abilities to make progress toward goals and personal changes. You may also need to leverage additional or external resources. While some people can lose ten pounds on their own, others might need a nutritionist or a personal trainer. There is nothing wrong with enlisting an expert to help you achieve your goals.

Relevant: If your goal is relevant, it is based on something significant and important to you. As discussed previously, it should also align with your deep beliefs and core values. Consider whether your stated goal will help you feel both fulfilled and content. You should also believe that the goal can be easily integrated into your life. Your goals are decidedly relevant if they bring out the best version of you!

Self-Esteem

Having confidence in your abilities and your value as a person is the heart of self-esteem. The relationship you have with your "self" — the essence of who you believe you are and how you see yourself — greatly influences how you see the world and others. It affects your acceptance (or nonacceptance) of poor treatment by others and your ability to set limits on what you will or will not accept. The reason I discuss self-esteem here is that goal achievement is the primary pathway to improving self-esteem and generally feeling good about yourself. You should create a goal that directly addresses aspects of your self-esteem — for example, a goal to alter your negative self-talk or beliefs. Understand that goal achievement is what's required to change the inner core of your relationship with your self.

Educating Yourself

Learn, read, listen to, talk about, research, and experience everything you can about the goal(s) you are trying to reach. There is so much information available to help you educate yourself, and much of it is available as part of formalized learning programs. There are books, workshops, e-courses, and so on available to help you and guide you in the direction of your goal. Don't be surprised if you need to learn some new skills to achieve your goal. The educational components are among the smaller steps you will take to achieve your goals.

Recovery

If you have been in unhealthy relationships, part of your goal planning must include a strategy for recovery. A dictionary definition of *recovery* is "a return to a normal state after a period of difficulty." I think the definition sums it up quite well. The word *recovery* is also used in the world of addiction. Someone in recovery is actively working a program to stay clean and sober or refrain from unhealthy compulsive behaviors. The word may feel stigmatizing, but I encourage you to stay open-minded to the general dictionary definition and how it applies to your love life. The elements of recovery are essential, and chapter 12 of this book is devoted to thoroughly exploring them.

Here's an example describing Leah's goal-setting strategy.

Leah is a twenty-nine-year-old woman. She is well educated and accomplished in her work. However, her love life is another story. She repeatedly finds herself with emotionally unavailable men. They are often the noncommittal or mama's-boy type. After her latest painful breakup, Leah sat down to write up her dating and relationship goals. Here's how hers look:

What is your goal, and why is it important?
To make better decisions about who I date, how long I stay in a relationship that I know is wrong for me. I also want to learn why I am making bad choices with men. This is important as I want to get married and have children one day with a compatible and reliable partner. I also do not want to be psychologically stuck. My goal aligns with my values because I hold myself accountable in the same way. I am a good person with a lot to offer, and I need someone who appreciates this and wants the same things I do.

What are the smaller action items that will help you reach your goal?

1. Find a good therapist to explore reasons for my choice and to keep me on track.

2. Talk more about my dating and relationship experiences with friends, and listen better to their advice, since they are more objective about it than I am.
3. Read several self-help books on this topic.
4. Get involved in a new hobby like photography, which I always wanted to do but did not dedicate enough time to. This will keep me more in balance.
5. Write up a list of qualities that are must-haves and a list of deal breakers in a potential partner.
6. Write positive affirmations on sticky notes to leave at different spots in my apartment to remind me of my goal efforts every day.
7. Start using a mindfulness app on my phone to be better able to tune in to my thoughts and feelings and develop self-awareness.

What is the time frame within which you hope to accomplish this goal?
I will begin working on the action steps today. I believe I can achieve this goal over the course of nine months to a year.

What will you do if you backslide or hit obstacles?
I will discuss any problems that block my work toward my goal with my therapist or my best friend (or both). I anticipate that I may make some mistakes, but I will be kinder to myself about them.

Being in Charge of Your Life (Not His)

Being in a relationship with an emotionally unavailable man can make your life seem out of control. If you want to take back your sense of control of your time, your love, and your life, you must believe that you are perfectly capable of being in control of yourself. A serious element of this will involve letting go of the idea that you can control your partner and focusing instead on managing your own reactions and behavior. Your goals should keep you focused on this track and motivated.

A goal without action isn't worth the paper it's written on. Taking action toward achieving a goal will take self-discipline. This is one of the most challenging aspects of having a goal. The self-discipline and motivation necessary to reach a goal involving your personal life is most certainly intrinsic. This means that it comes from the inside out. You will not win a fancy car or get paid anything for making personal changes. However, what you do get is both intangible and priceless. You will get the relationship you deserve and are entitled to. The consequences of *not* making changes will be the ongoing pain and despair you feel.

As you work toward your goals, you will reach many points at which you must make decisions. Every decision will have a consequence that will propel you either forward or backward. Other people in your life, even those who say they are supportive, may resist your efforts once they see the impact of the changes you are making. Here are some examples:

- You realize you must work on your personal boundaries. Your mother is very happy for you, given that she sees what she calls your "relationship disasters." But part of your plan involves creating better boundaries with her as well. When you reduce the amount of time you spend with her and decline to give full details about your dating and social activities, she gets upset. The positive changes you are making inadvertently affect her as well but are necessary in order for you to grow.
- After you break up with your emotionally unavailable

boyfriend for what seems like the umpteenth time, he tries to reach out to you again. You usually resist for a few days (sometimes only hours) and then call him back; but this time, you instantly delete the message and block his number. He pops into the store where you work to kick up his efforts. He's not used to this and becomes agitated at your firm "no" and your request that he leave immediately.

- You meet someone new who asks to spend the day with you. You are superexcited because this guy seems great. In the past, you would drop everything and go. But now that you have new goals and standards for yourself, you decide to go to the yoga class you signed up for and later meet an old friend for lunch. The guy is disappointed but understands that you have prior commitments.
- Your friends know you are always willing to go out and party with them. You have decided to cut back on going out to save money but also to take an online course that requires a significant amount of time and energy. Your friends verbalized a lot of support for making the personal changes you told them about. However, now they realize what those changes really mean — less time with them.

The best way to respond to the resistance of others is to avoid returning to old ways of thinking and acting. You should slow down to become fully aware of the consequences of your choices and concentrate on them for a while. How will different scenarios play out? What behaviors will remind you of your old habits? What actions will align with the goals you set? Understand and prepare for the fact that others may be disappointed or upset by your choices (even when they are healthy choices!). Doing so will keep you in control of your life, and it will let you *feel* as if you are in control of your life.

Stay Motivated

Creating a goal to keep you focused will help motivate you to make changes. However, we all know that it can be challenging to stay motivated. Here are a few additional strategies that can help motivate you.

Use Visualization

Visualization is about forming a mental image of success. Allow yourself complete freedom to dream and fantasize about yourself in a thriving and successful place in the future. You can also visualize where you were previously and how far you have come. This is a cognitive technique that lets you use your imagination to realize an outcome you wish to achieve. The exercise can be purely mental, but some prefer to write down their visualized thoughts or create a "vision board" with various images pasted on it that represent their visualizations. You can visualize in an intentional way by meditating or setting aside time to do it. Or you may do it at random when you are moved to do so, just letting your mind wander. The focus should be an image of yourself achieving whatever it is you wish to achieve in your relationships and work life. Visualizing creates a more concrete reminder of what you want for your future. You should be visualizing daily what it will look like when you have reached your goal or goals.

Find Role Models

Whom do you know who has already been successful at doing what you are trying to accomplish? Who in your real life inspires you? Spend more time with these people, and perhaps even pick their brains for information. The people you surround yourself with can play a vital role in determining whether you succeed or fail at achieving your goals. Avoid pessimistic and negative people. If you have too few role models around, it is entirely acceptable to find inspirational celebrities, writers, artists, speakers, and others in the public eye.

Continually Seek Out Motivating Material

There is a plethora of books, quotes, websites, Facebook groups, videos, TEDx Talks, and so on that are motivational in nature. Exposing yourself to positive and affirming personal stories and ideas from others will shift your mind-set in that direction and continually give you needed boosts when your motivation is waning. You can also do something as deliberate as placing Post-it notes with positive affirmations or quotes where you will see them every day.

By now, you can see why being goal-oriented is instrumental in getting the love and life you want. Keep in mind that your goals can be altered or reassessed at your discretion. You may realize that a goal must be broken down even further into achievable parts, or that you must integrate a new component that you didn't think of at first. Focus more on the *process* of goal achievement, and less on the *outcome*. Give yourself permission to get off course without punishing yourself by being excessively self-critical. In fact, develop a few strategies to counteract potential pitfalls or blocks while you are creating your goals. Goal creation is meant to move you forward with clarity and confidence; it doesn't demand perfection. The next few chapters will continue to guide you in that direction.

CHAPTER ELEVEN

HAVING A HEALTHY RELATIONSHIP

Working with couples day in and day out, helping them with their problems, has given me a bird's-eye view of the struggles they have while trying to make love work. Love isn't always easy! One of the most common situations I see is partners unhappy over something that existed before they committed to each other. This may be undesirable personality traits, a poor temperament, bad behavior, addiction, and so on. People seem willing to commit to a person with such traits and behaviors anyway, even when these are extremely problematic. In fact, this happens all the time! Therefore, in this chapter I will "reverse engineer" — in a sense, work backward from — what I see occurring within distressed marriages. By discussing it, I hope to save you future heartache. I want to help you follow the number one rule when it comes to relationships: choose wisely and carefully!

Dating

Dating is confusing! Many men and women aren't sure how to "properly" date. They are often too invested in the *outcome* right off the bat and fail to do what it takes to find out whether the person sitting across from them is the right (or woefully wrong) fit. Often a lack of accountability in the dating process allows people to act without necessarily thinking about the impact they are having on others. Moreover, dating has become mystifying in the digital age. Technology has further complicated the dating process, perhaps decreasing accountability even more. And it is tough to get a read on people through text. It is also frustrating to know that someone is glued to his phone and knows you are trying to reach him, yet he finds a way to ignore you. I also think conversation has become a lost art. Despite all this, it is necessary to discern sooner rather than later whether someone is a potential match.

Given the mixed signals and confusion, it is worthwhile to explore how to approach the process of dating, especially if you are seeking long-term commitment. Let's discuss some dating do's and don'ts, not only to make your dating efforts more successful, but also to help you learn to detect potential emotional unavailability from the get-go.

Dating Do's

- Do be clear in your head about your dating goals. Are you just looking for a hookup, or do you want to find a long-term relationship or marriage?
- Do make sure your life is fulfilling in many other ways, independently of the status of your romantic life.
- Do assume that you will have dates that go poorly, and

that you will meet people who you're not attracted to or who are totally wrong for you. It goes with the territory. Be open-minded and optimistic about dating.

- Do decide if you prefer to be chased or if you don't mind doing the chasing. But be prepared for this to probably never change. So, if you are chasing, but you hope your date will catch on and chase you, understand that it is not likely to happen.
- Do pay attention to actions much, much more than to words.
- Do keep dating other people until you know you have a keeper and have had the "exclusivity talk." Many women do a "one guy at a time" strategy, and it's not always a good one.
- Do focus on compatibility and values that are in sync, instead of chemistry or physical attraction.
- Do be very careful with online dating. Unfortunately, people are more apt to lie, to really be looking for a hookup, or to approach dating like a "sport," with multiple dates going all the time, without intending to have a relationship. On the other hand, online dating significantly increases your ability to meet someone you would not typically meet.
- Do be very, very cautious if you immediately feel:
  - a strong sexual attraction or chemistry
  - like you want to help/rescue/save him
  - like you want to mother him
  - he is similar to all your terrible exes
- Do listen closely and believe what your date tells you! Many will give you all the information you need to know on the first date.

Dating Don'ts

- Don't be quick to blame yourself if he acts like a jerk.
- Don't date if you are not in a good place emotionally or are in the midst of a personal crisis (for example, a recent loss, a divorce, and so on).
- Don't buy into the soul mate mentality. There are many potential matches out there for you.
- Don't date people who are "geographically undesirable." Stick with prospects you can get to know face-to-face.
- Don't get caught up in overanalyzing the date or wondering what he thinks of you. Instead, ask yourself what *you* think of him.
- Don't immediately discard the "boring" date or the one you are not super attracted to. You may have a diamond in the rough. You may have someone you just need more time to get to know. You may have a real, live emotionally available man!

Try to have a few phone calls with a potential date. Don't endlessly text and not set up a call or a meeting. If you have a few initial phone conversations that go well, it's better to meet sooner rather than later. I understand this is time-consuming, but some potential dates will have fantastic chemistry with you over the phone or by text but will somehow flop in person.

The first date should be something low-pressure and casual. If you met online, going for coffee is ideal. Avoid going to a bar or otherwise drinking alcohol on the first date. You want to have all your wits about you. If it's someone you already know, and he suggests lunch or dinner, go for it. The primary reason you are meeting at all is to determine if this person is well suited to you. This information will come from the conversations you have and the behaviors you witness. Therefore, what you do on the date, whether you have coffee or lunch, is less important than what you see and hear from the person you are sitting across from.

Heather found it refreshing that, after meeting Trevor online, he was direct and asked to meet her after a bit of texting and an initial phone conversation. She was very interested in him based on what she knew about him so far — he looked great on paper. She felt let down, though, when she met him in person. He was a bit less attractive than in his online photo, so there weren't any butterflies in her stomach. She decided she would just politely get through the date and go on to the next guy soon enough.

Things suddenly took a turn toward the end of their evening when Trevor got an unexpected call on his cell phone, which he excused himself to take. Heather thought this was odd, but when he came back to the table, he began to tell her about his volunteer work as a Big Brother mentor. It was his mentee who had called him to get some quick advice on a problem. He talked about spending every Saturday morning coaching basketball for boys who lack male role models and live in poverty. She couldn't believe her ears: this high-level executive was dedicating time to helping others in this way. Heather decided not to focus on the lack of immediate chemistry. She knew she really liked who this guy was and wanted to know more.

Many women turn their noses up at good-hearted, stable, and consistent guys like Trevor. Without the immediate flood of physical attraction and chemistry, they think the person could not possibly be a match. Don't make this mistake! Ignoring red flags (and dissing the green flags) will keep you in perpetual relationship misery.

In the Beginning

Let's say the first date went well, and you get asked out again. The first month or two is when you will determine whether this person is still a match and whether he meets your criteria. You should know the difference between charming quirks you can deal with and deep-seated character flaws that will leave you in turmoil. You also must boldly speak your mind: talk about your intentions and what is important to you. This is a tricky thing to do when you are also worried about what your date thinks of you. I advise you to worry less about him and more about yourself. Not thinking about yourself, your values, and your goals for the future may let you continue making poor choices among prospective partners.

Although it feels natural to do so, don't ever rush into love. Don't become a victim of the sense of urgency that comes with infatuation. I'm talking about the feeling that, if you don't hurry the relationship, it may disappear. If this is the person you are meant to be with, he will not suddenly vanish if you take it slow. Yes, there are exceptions to this rule. We have all heard at least one story about a person who met someone, instantly fell in love, got married three weeks later, and marched off into the sunset to live happily ever after. However, the more likely scenario is that the relationship tanks because you took things too fast. You also do not want to fall prey to someone who "love bombs" you with romantic intensity, only to ghost you later. Allow a relationship to flourish gradually, to save yourself from potential heartache.

There are many benefits to a slow, gradual ramp-up that are worth discussing. As explained in chapter 6 about love, the rational part of your brain is offline. It takes tremendous effort to exercise some restraint and not give in to impulses. It is hard, but not impossible, to maintain your rationality and keep what you have learned about yourself and your proclivities in the forefront of your mind. Having explored your family history in chapter 5, you will have a strong sense of why you behave in particular ways when dating and in romantic relationships. Think actively about what you need and want, and show courage in articulating those things to someone who may become part of your life. Develop clarity about your values and allow them to guide your decisions about potential partners. You must also be prepared to go in a different direction if you see that a potential partner is not aligned with your values and needs.

Your time is valuable, and you should be protective of it. There's no need to brush aside your work, hobbies, and friendships when a new person comes into your life. Once you get too out of balance, you may seriously struggle to rebalance yourself later on. Putting all your "emotional eggs" in one basket is never a sound idea. Maintain your sense of individuality and independence while you are integrating a potential romantic partner into your life. This person should comfortably fit into your life, and you should comfortably fit into his.

Early Dating Questions

Slowing down and dating mindfully requires you to tune in to your heart and gut during the dating process. Avoid getting caught up in romantic feelings that block you from reflecting upon your date and how you both related to each other. Here are some questions to ask yourself when you start dating someone new:

1. Do I like this person?
2. Was my date polite and respectful to me and others?
3. Do our values and agendas line up so far?

4. Is there anything about this person that made me un-comfortable?
5. Does this person respond in a reasonable amount of time when I reach out?
6. Are there any obvious yellow or red flags?
7. What is my gut telling me about this person?
8. Did my date say or do anything strange or off-putting?
9. Is the chemistry super strong?
10. Did he pressure me for sex or anything else I did not wish to do?

The Timing of Sex

There is no absolutely right or wrong answer to the question of when to have sex, but I have one caveat. Wait awhile if you desire a long-term relationship and not just a hookup. You need to ask yourself how you would feel if the person never called you again after sex. If you are hoping that the sex will deepen his commitment level, you are mistaken. You are much better off having sex *after* you see several other behaviors that line up with commitment beforehand! Don't think sex will solidify your status without explicit confirmation that this is the case and without deep trust between you.

Sexual desire and intimacy are regularly seen as signs that a new relationship is going in the right direction — essentially as signals telling you that "this person likes me" and is investing himself in the relationship. We frequently look for ways to soothe our attachment anxiety when we are romantically interested, and seeking reassurance though sex is a popular channel for this. However, there may be gender differences in this regard. Some research findings indicate that women's displays of desire early in a romantic relationship may actually be viewed by men as threatening! Men may emotionally detach themselves in response to such behavior to defend against feeling vulnerable. So understand that the outcome of being sexual early in a relationship may be the opposite of what you intended, since it can interfere with a man's ability to form a secure attachment. When men are the initiators of intimate sexual contact, it improves the chance of a secure bond building. You still have the power to decide what is right or not right for you. Women usually need much more than just physical interactions to feel safe and secure. They need the emotional level as well. It seems that developing closeness on an emotional and intellectual level first is a better direction to go in an emerging relationship.

There is a confusing paradox in relationships with emotionally unavailable men: the sex can be really good even if the relationship is bad. If you have a significant amount of sexual chemistry with a man who is not entirely invested in you, having sex with him may become a high that you continually seek — anything to feel good, anything to cling to the fantasy that he will eventually be all yours. Often, the passion and intensity of the sex are intoxicating, keeping you in an addictive state. Understand that, if you carved out the sexual part of the relationship, you would have little or no substance. This is not true of mutual intimacy.

If you use sex as a method of showing your love and keeping the relationship going, you're operating on the false assumption that sex will make him love and need you. You also might be much more concerned about your partner's sexual gratification than your own. It's important to realize that behaving this way in a relationship can be seen as manipulative: you are using sex to keep your partner interested. A lot of energy goes into the physicality of the relationship. You likely confuse the excitement around these sexual power plays with love. As you can see, though, there is no discourse about the *real* problems in the relationship. Under the surface remains a fractured bond.

Self-Disclosure

It's tempting to "sell" yourself, to unintentionally overinflate yourself in a way that will be hard to keep up. On the other hand, you may not disclose enough of the vital information that your date needs about you. We often idealize those we have romantic feelings for, and we present an idealized picture of ourselves. It is challenging but necessary to strike a balance between what you reveal and what you keep close to the vest for a while. Sharing too much to soon can make someone see you as needy, overeager, or helpless, or it can otherwise imply that something is "off" about you. Focusing on quelling your fear of rejection, rather than on the quality and mutuality of the interaction, will yield a poor outcome.

If you find yourself spilling your guts right away or continuously oversharing, you must examine your motives. Maybe you are doing it for some self-serving reason. Give yourself the "WAIT" test: Ask yourself, "Why am I talking?" Your answer should help you decide if it's okay to continue sharing or if you should pull back a bit. The sharing should be reciprocal: numerous small moments between the two of you that build trust and enable you to take emotional risks with each other.

When it comes to self-disclosure, how do you find a balance? There should be an easy flow of conversation that allows space for who you are to naturally emerge. The disclosures between the two of you should flow back and forth. Don't dodge opportunities for meaningful self-disclosure. It can be a tremendous relief to have someone know your embarrassing truths and still want to continue to be with you and learn more. But there is no need to "vomit" this all out within the first few dates. There is, however a need to be loved and accepted for who you genuinely are before making a serious commitment. You should expect your potential partner to feel exactly the same way. No one likes being lied to or to feel like a fool because secrets were kept. You are imperfect, and that's okay!

On the flip side, be wary of someone who makes you feel like you can't share at all. If you get a negative vibe or under-handed insults in response to what you say, alarm bells should be ringing. Do not plan to continue a relationship with anyone who shows you early on that he already rejects the essence of who you are as a person or if he refuses to share in a mutual way.

Red Flags (and Yellow Flags)

The ideal way to avoid getting too deep into a relationship with someone emotionally unavailable and incapable of intimacy is to recognize the red flags early on. Some flags may indicate caution, but others scream "RUN!"

Do not ignore these flags when dating:

- Rudeness to anyone. The most obvious red flag is your date being rude or even nasty to service people you interact with while together.
- Inappropriate social behavior or disregard for social norms — for example, telling crude jokes, excessive cursing, taking things that don't belong to him, parking illegally, failing to tip, and so on.
- Drinking too much.
- Pushing you to do anything you don't want to do, especially sex.
- Displaying a jealous streak.

- Pushing for commitment early.
- Telling you every single ex of his is crazy.
- Telling you how perfect you are.
- Game-playing or inconsistently showing interest in you.
- Showing indifference to your interests, work, and hobbies or, worse, scoffing at or criticizing them.
- Talking only about himself.
- Being perpetually and unapologetically late.
- Not taking you on proper dates and, instead, expecting you to just come over and hang out.
- Being secretive or heavily guarded about disclosing information about himself.
- Being capable of only small talk or superficial conversations.
- Having a sense of humor that is excessively sarcastic, biting, or teasing.
- Taking more than an hour or two to return a text or call.
- Readily texting you (or sexting you), while seemingly unable to ever make plans to get together.
- Never offering to pay on a date.
- Mentioning things about yourself that he thinks you should work on.
- Sending mixed signals.
- Telling you how hard it is for him to keep a job (and he doesn't know why). Alternatively, he has frequently been fired or is chronically unemployed.
- Your friends do not like him.

Your Tribe

Thoroughly check out any potential romantic partner before investing too much time in him. You can do this initially by being mindful of any red flags that come up. Determining if someone is a match is an ongoing process — until you see that everything aligns, giving you the green light to move forward. Those you trust and rely on in your social circle — your tribe, so to speak — must be part of your process. This includes your friends and family and perhaps older, wiser confidantes. Get the perspectives of same-sex and opposite-sex friends (or their partners) and find out what they are picking up about your date. Seek honest opinions about anything they noticed — about how your date treats you, how comfortable you both seem with each other, whether they can picture you with this person, and anything else that is relevant. You must maintain an open mind and avoid defensiveness during these discussions.

This is what Ava did after starting to date Luke. She was really taken with him. He was handsome, smart, and funny. They had much in common, including their religious beliefs. They had even grown up in the same neighborhood but had never met until two months earlier. The only red flag she could pick up on was his occasional aloofness and lame excuses for not returning her calls or texts in a reasonable amount of time. Otherwise, things seemed to be going well. She was glad when she got invited to a party some good friends were throwing; she would be able to introduce Luke to them. In the meantime, she told them all about him and how much she liked him.

They went to the party and had a great time, and Ava couldn't wait to debrief her friends the next day. She was disheartened to learn that they were not as taken as she was with Luke. In fact, Luke had actually hit on one of her friends at the party. Another girlfriend let her know that her boyfriend thought he was sleazy. Luke had made a crude joke about Ava behind her back. He had also bragged frequently to others at the party, and they were not impressed. Ava's love goggles were ripped off. She could not reconcile what she knew about Luke and what her friends were saying. But given her dating history, she wanted to pay attention to what others could see that she couldn't. Rather than getting mad, she appreciated her friends for their honesty. She took a big step back from Luke and focused on other men who showed interest in dating her.

Attachment in Dating

You will likely recall from previous chapters that both dating and romantic relationships can set off your attachment-alarm bells. Those who are emotionally unavailable tend to have the avoidant style. Those who have an anxious style are inclined to find themselves pulled into a dance with someone avoidant. This gravitational force is a pervasive one. It is part of a pattern that often lands a couple in therapy together when they reach a breaking point in a long-term relationship. Avoidantly attached individuals seem to be naturally drawn to anxiously attached individuals, because such a relationship confirms their internal view of self ("I don't need anyone") and others ("People are weak and dependent"). In some cases, even a person with a secure style may find herself caught up with an avoidant. If you have an anxious style, when you are triggered you will protest the disconnection, often by escalating emotionally. Those with an avoidant style use deactivating strategies (behaviors to create distance) to "turn down" their need for intimacy and connection when triggered. It makes sense that the seesaw or roller-coaster pattern can crop up readily in the anxious-avoidant pairing.

The field of neuroscience informs us that our brains naturally scan for "danger" in romantic relationships. This means you are alert to threats to the relationship that affect connection, intimacy, and closeness. When you have a date with someone with a secure attachment style, you will not sense these threats. Your date will be calm and predictable. You should not confuse attachment system activation with love, as many people do. When there are no immediate alarms or bells and whistles, your brain may not "code" it as love. Securely attached people have a positive mind-set about intimacy and relationships. They expect things to work out for them in the end. They anticipate meeting their match and falling in love.

Here are some characteristics of those who are securely attached and emotionally healthy:

- They don't play games or give mixed signals.
- They know how to discuss thoughts and feelings.
- They are capable of empathy.
- They are direct and honest when they talk to you.
- They know how to speak openly and freely.
- They enjoy doing things independently as well as together.
- They know how to apologize as well as forgive.
- They are comfortable with closeness.
- They know that physical and emotional intimacy go hand in hand.
- They treat you with kindness and respect.
- They are sensitive to your feelings.
- They aim to engage in problem-solving and improve the relationship.
- They know how to fight fair.
- They don't create distance when you move in for closeness.
- They react and respond rationally in the relationship.
- If they don't want to be with you, they will tell you directly and sensitively.

It's probably not surprising to hear that those with secure attachment styles most often end up in happy and prosperous relationships. The good news is that your attachment style is not set in stone. It can be reshaped throughout your life. It can change in a positive or negative way, depending on the partner you are with. Therefore, you will have the best chance of growing in a secure direction yourself if you pick as secure a partner as possible. Alternatively, you can choose a partner who at the very least recognizes his own insecure pattern and wants to grow and change with you.

Recall from chapter 6 that the process of developing a secure style through your interactions with others, and in the context of your romantic relationship, is called earned security. Making sense of and reconciling your FOO experiences, as laid out in chapter 5, is a big component of the movement toward earned security. Being open to and embracing an emotionally available partner can help change your internal negative template into a very positive one. New experiences and possibilities will become part of your new narrative. With this new lens, you will learn to trust that a reliable and consistent person (like a spouse or partner) will be there for you in your times of distress — the very opposite of what you may have learned in childhood and past relationships. The road to earned security is a challenging one with much risk-taking and vulnerability, but it can bring you the kind of love you have always wanted. The reward is well worth the work, because an *earned* secure attachment style can change your life and your relationships for the better, permanently.

Empathy and Attunement

The development of trust in a relationship is highly dependent upon two core concepts: empathy and attunement. These

concepts are the antidotes to the bad dating and relationship behavior (such as ghosting) that leaves you frustrated. Attunement
is about being deeply aware of yourself and others. It is also
about being receptive to information you get from others. When
two people are attuned to each other, there is emotional awareness, responsiveness, and empathy. Someone who is attuned
and empathic to others would not ghost, cushion, breadcrumb,
or engage in other bad dating and relationship behaviors.

An empathetic person is sensitive to your feelings and can
"walk in your shoes." He is respectful of your viewpoint. Even
if it differs from his, he can validate your feelings or attitudes
as reasonable and understandable. He will demonstrate tolerance for your perspective without defensiveness, harsh judgment, or criticism.

Whether you are dating or in an ongoing relationship, a
man who is attuned to how his behavior affects you, who can
show empathy and validate your experience, is a keeper! This is
the type of person who would not treat you poorly, because he
is aware of how it feels to be treated this way. He would respond
thoughtfully and appropriately if he realized he had hurt you.
This does not mean you will never be hurt or misunderstood.
It does mean that your partner can lean into the relationship,
apologize if necessary, and show concern for having hurt
you. This occasional "rupture and repair" interaction is common in all relationships. I emphasize the word *occasional* —
as in "not the usual." The norm is *not* to be constantly hurt
and frustrated, but hurt and frustration do happen sometimes.
The difference lies in how your partner handles it.

Trust

Trust is earned. You do not have to, nor should you, trust
someone implicitly when you first meet. This does not mean

you are suspicious of that person's intentions. What it does mean is that you do what we do in the American justice system: assume that someone is innocent until proven guilty. Your mind remains open, receptive to the signs that someone is trustworthy or not. You pay close attention to words and actions to see if the "trust meter" rises or falls. If it falls, you should not keep trying to cement a relationship with this person (even if you believe you are in love with him).

The needle on the trust meter will rise when your partner is:

- predictable
- reliable
- consistent
- accountable
- protective
- willing to keep your best interests (not just his) at heart
- willing to confide in you about all aspects of his life
- open to learning
- well thought of in his social circle
- caring and concerned when he has hurt you

The Healthy Relationship

Healthy and successful relationships have several core characteristics in common. These relationships are defined by the couple's sense of safety and security, empathy for each other, responsiveness to the other's needs, and attitude of we-ness. Each partner is attuned to the other, and they both openly communicate. There is a profound understanding and awareness of each other. They count on each other and believe firmly that each has the other's back. They also take emotional risks with each other — they are not afraid to be vulnerable. They have the courage to show each other who they really are. Trust and safety is built slowly and gradually from the beginning of the relationship. In fact, this trust and safety is the foundation the relationship is built on. When it isn't there at the start, the relationship is built on a faulty foundation and often never fully recovers.

If this is hard to imagine, look around for role models engaged in healthy and secure relationships. Think about those in your life currently or in the past. How do these couples treat each other? How do they interact with each other, the world, and those around them? What seems to make their bond solid? You can also reflect upon the way that healthy and secure people interact with you. How do they avoid drama and toxic behavior? How do they handle conflict and challenges in life? How do they respond to you when you are having trouble? It is likely you do know several such people and couples who can help you see that healthy relationships are possible!

In a healthy relationship, there is open, assertive, and effective communication. There are no games. Communication is clear and direct. When healthy couples get stuck or start arguing, they tend to address what is underneath the surface. When attachment-based triggers are activated in such situations, an emotionally unavailable partner will typically use deactivating strategies — distancing thoughts and actions — that cause him to turn away when you need him the most. An emotionally available partner will express his fears, longings, and vulnerabilities to you instead of shutting you out. In turn, it will feel safe for you to do the same. When partners tap into their vulnerabilities and share them, they can come together to work through the problem. They can both use coping skills to effectively reduce their reactivity and overwhelming emotions so that they can stay present and engaged with each other and talk calmly. When partners communicate in a healthy way, they are able to get back on stable ground relatively quickly after an argument. Their equilibrium returns, and they carry on without holding grudges.

Emotional Intelligence

Some of the characteristics of healthy relationships described in this chapter embody what is known as *emotional intelligence*. Emotional intelligence is about being adept in several core areas involving emotion within yourself and in your interactions with others. The areas of personal competence include self-awareness and management of both your emotions and your behaviors in response to them. Accurately perceiving your own emotions and positively channeling those emotions are key to becoming personally and socially competent.

The other component of emotional intelligence is how accurately you tune in to the emotions of those around you and assess what might be going on with them, and whether you use this knowledge efficaciously to mediate your interactions with them. As you can imagine, emotional intelligence is something you want to develop and something you want to look for in a partner. Emotionally intelligent people experience much more successful platonic and romantic relationships, greater academic achievement, more positive interactions with their children, and greater success at work.

Because emotional intelligence is such an important component of a healthy relationship, I've made a list of skills, traits, and abilities commonly found in people who possess a high level of emotional intelligence:

- optimism
- insight
- motivation

- strong vocabulary and an ability to verbalize emotional experience
- empathy
- ability to regulate emotion
- assertive communication
- forgiving nature
- good social skills
- curiosity about others
- ability to have fun
- unlikely to become offended
- ability to cope with rejection
- confidence

A lot seems to ride on our having emotional intelligence! It is impossible for every person to possess everything on this list, so don't be discouraged. Take an inventory of what you believe you are good at and what may need some more development. Feedback from others can also be beneficial, since we sometimes don't see our shortcomings clearly.

Interpersonal Regulation

In chapter 8 you learned about self-regulation of emotion. When you are interacting with another person, the two of you will experience varying degrees of something termed *interpersonal regulation* of emotion. This type of emotional regulation emerges when you are trying to influence another person in order to reach a goal. This often includes influencing this person's feelings or thoughts. For example, when you sense distance between yourself and your partner, and you seek reassurance of his ongoing interest in you, you are engaging in an interpersonal regulation tactic. If you are interacting with someone emotionally unavailable and/or you have an anxious attachment style, you will tend to emphasize closeness, intimacy, connection. Your efforts will collide with those of someone who values autonomy and distance. It is essential for you and your partner to find a way to balance conflicting needs so that you are both satisfied with the relationship. Both preferences are valid, but when there are extreme differences in two people's goals — the goal of emphasizing closeness, intimacy, and connection on the one hand, and autonomy and distance on the other — conflict and dissatisfaction will result. Partners with a secure and healthy relationship do not view these goals as incompatible. They remain flexible and find ways to balance and coordinate them.

Finding "the one" is not an easy task, and there is no substantial research that provides us with a magic formula. There is no way to find love and not get hurt in the process, either. There are things, though, that can help make this endeavor easier by improving your odds and minimizing heartache.

In your search for love, you will be rejected (at least once!). You will also never be fully satisfied with any reason you are given for being rejected. Moreover, you will reject other people you meet. You may find someone to take a chance on, someone you believe has "potential." But if you keep trying to change someone to fit the mold of what you desire, and it isn't working, examine your motives and behavior. You must be realistic about a partner's willingness to change. Don't keep trying harder to fix him. Instead, move on and declare yourself open to finding someone capable of reciprocating love. There is nothing like sharing your life with a partner you can count on, one who is emotionally available to you and more than willing to love you back.

CHAPTER TWELVE

PROFESSIONAL HELP AND RECOVERY

It may have crossed your mind at some point in your life journey to consider getting professional help. Someone may have even suggested it to you. Unfortunately, the idea of getting help for a mental health–related problem is still stigmatized by some people. But the vast majority of people who get past the difficulty of asking for and getting help are usually relieved they did so and look back on their initial reluctance as senseless and misdirected. I can offer some general guidance to assist you in answering the question of whether you *need* help. But regardless of your impressions after these considerations, I urge you to welcome the opportunity for personal growth and deep, meaningful changes in your life and relationships, in the form of guidance, support, or psychotherapy from a skilled professional.

Considering Psychotherapy

You should strongly consider psychotherapy from a licensed professional for any of the following circumstances.

❏ You are concerned about behaviors and thoughts you can't seem to stop on your own.

❏ You believe your feelings and behavior are getting worse over time.

❏ You do not have a good support system.

❏ You rely on, or burden, others too much with your problems.

❏ You have not been able to make desired changes on your own.

❏ Your problems seem to be affecting your sleep, ability to concentrate, and/or eating habits.

❏ You struggle to maintain healthy relationships with others in addition to romantic partners.

❏ Your mood is often down, or up and down.

❏ You sometimes use drugs or alcohol to help your mood or to cope with negative thoughts and situations.

❏ You have had several stressful events in a short period of time.

❏ You have thoughts of self-harm or thoughts that you would be better off dead.

Therapy has come a long, long way since the days of Freud and psychoanalysis. Therapy is often shorter-term now, lasting anywhere from a few months to a year, and is nonpathologizing. This means that therapists do not view their clients through the lens of disease or abnormality. Instead, they are looking to find out "What happened to you?" and not simply "What's wrong with you?" Therapists may have to assign you a diagnosis in order to bill your insurance or satisfy some other external expectation, but most contemporary therapists are much less concerned with a diagnosis than with helping you in a holistic way to reach good health and happiness. A diagnosis is also helpful when medication is required to treat certain symptoms. Otherwise, therapy focuses on your goals and on providing an outside, objective point of view in a nonjudgmental way. There are also specialized approaches designed to laser-focus on a specific problem (or problems), whether it's unhealthy relationships, trauma, addiction, or any other issue. Many therapists who have developed niche practices dedicated to a particular population or problem are also passionate about their work.

There are several ways to find and choose a therapist. You should initially consider what you can afford, if you must use your private insurance, and when you can regularly fit therapy into your schedule. Searching the internet is a popular way to find a therapist, but a personal recommendation is best. After an initial visit with your chosen therapist, you should feel that you can be candid with this professional, and that he or she understands your view of the problem and has the skills to help you. You can make a change if you don't feel that this person is a match after a session or two. Understand that your commitment to and motivation for the treatment will be instrumental in determining how well it works for you. The therapist will guide you to help *yourself* and should not be working harder than you are. Therapy is also a *process*: your goals are reached over time, and the progression is not always a straight one. There is often an uptick in pain, discomfort, and negative feelings at the beginning that are then worked through during the course of the therapeutic journey and re-lationship with your therapist.

Another form of help comes from coaches. These professionals often focus on helping you with your life, dating, work, or relationships. A coach may be the right option for you, but only if you do not require deep psychological and interpersonal changes. Coaches are generally useful for people functioning adequately but not meeting their full potential. They motivate them and help them stay on target with their goals. Coaches do not delve deeply into making connections between your early experiences and current behavior. They also do not treat depression, anxiety, destructive behavior patterns, trauma, or severe mood disorders. There are no licensing or educational requirements for coaches. This does not mean there are not some excellent coaches who can be very helpful. But it does mean that if you really need therapy to meet your goals, then a coach may not be sufficient. A therapist can also coach as well, but a coach cannot do therapy.

If you have decided to seek out a professional therapist to address repetitive relationship patterns, what licensing and clinical experience should you look for? At a minimum, the therapist should have a state license. This requires at least a master's degree and often two or more years under clinical supervision before passing an exam and becoming licensed. You may also seek someone licensed at the doctoral level (PhD or PsyD). I strongly recommend that you choose a person with foundational experience in all of these areas: family and couple dynamics, attachment, FOO work, and trauma. You will want to select an "evidence-based" form of therapy that has been subjected to numerous studies demonstrating good outcomes.

Therapists are often eclectic, meaning one therapist may draw from several approaches. You do not have to know the names of these psychological interventions, but if it is important to you, here are some of the ones that will help you with relational problems:

- **Emotionally focused couples' therapy:** Designed for the treatment of couples with negative communication patterns and/or emotional disconnection within the relationship. This approach is focused on the science of love, bonding, and attachment. It has also expanded into the realm of treating individuals and families.

- **Accelerated experiential-dynamic psychotherapy:** Focuses on healing emotional and relational experiences, as well as on transforming behavior through in-depth processing of difficult past experiences.

- **Cognitive-behavioral therapy:** Designed to treat couples and/or individuals by challenging distorted thoughts and beliefs as well as unhelpful behaviors. This approach has an educational and structured foundation that emphasizes thoughts and behavior instead of feelings.

- **Trauma-informed care** and/or **eye-movement desensitization and reprocessing (EMDR):** These are therapeutic approaches that address trauma.

- **Mindfulness-based stress reduction** or **acceptance and commitment therapy:** Designed to teach mindfulness meditation and/or how to integrate mindfulness into everyday life, and it is often mixed with behavior analysis or cognitive therapy.

There is one last critically important element of therapy that I stress here. Your therapist can be a stable and consistent person you develop trust with in a way you may never have been able to do previously. In that context, your therapist can become a positive attachment figure and "co-regulator" of your emotional experiences. One's emotional arousal and re-activity (triggers) can at times become heightened out of proportion to a situation. And depending on how severe this is, the therapist, particularly if he or she has an attachment orientation, can help facilitate changes in the safe environment of his or her office. A therapist can also help you develop a coherent narrative of your relationship and family history. We touched on the idea of the earned security that can occur in a romantic relationship, but it can also happen in the therapeutic relationship. For many who have sought psychotherapy, their relationship with their therapist (and within the sanctity of the therapist's office) has been pivotal and life changing.

Group Therapy and Self-Help Groups

Group therapy is a gathering led by a mental health professional that includes two or more people working on similar problems. People often participate in group therapy in addition to individual therapy or medication treatment. These groups are usually either *process-oriented* or *psychoeducation-oriented*. In process groups, the experience of therapy becomes the focus. They are helpful when you are trying to get feedback about how you are viewed by others. These groups provide a great opportunity to develop self-awareness, self-confidence, and a sense of belonging. In a process group, there is also a possibility of developing more insight, behavior changes, or healing, in relation to early family dynamics. Psychoeducation groups are professionally led, and place more emphasis on teaching about a topic, problem, or skill. The therapist is more directive and sometimes engages the group in activities or exercises.

Another form of help is the self-help group, also called a support group, such as Alcoholics Anonymous and Al-Anon.

Self-help groups are not led by a therapist; instead, the members provide mutual support to each other. The group members all share a common problem and the goal of healing and recovering from the problem. By disclosing your thoughts and feelings on the problem and how it affects you, you learn to feel you are not alone and that others are there to help you.

Many people are fearful about attending a group to address their problems. Despite this, group therapy and group support are often tremendously helpful to people who are trying to make changes. When loneliness or pain sets in as a result of your involvement with an emotionally unavailable person, the connection you experience from other group members can go a very long way toward helping you meet your goals.

Trauma

The impact of trauma can show up in a host of relationship problems. When coupled with an emotionally unresponsive or abusive romantic partner, trauma survivors often re-create and relive childhood experiences and other early experiences. They may have an unconscious drive to correct these experiences or a sense of familiarity with the toxicity of it all. Left unhealed, trauma wreaks havoc on your intimate relationships. It is not uncommon, however, to fail to realize one is experiencing the impact of trauma on one's life and relationships. Let's explore what trauma is and what you must focus on to break free of its grip.

Trauma comes from experiencing a deeply disturbing event (or events) that invades your sense of control and safety. Your capacity to integrate the experience into your current reality is impaired. We usually associate trauma with those who have experienced combat, war, terrorism, sexual assault, or catastrophic accidents. These are frequently debilitating and profoundly disturbing; however, smaller everyday events accumulating over time can also create trauma. Some professionals distinguish between "big-T trauma," such as war or rape, and "little-t trauma," such as enduring poverty or family dysfunction during childhood. These events are often known as adverse childhood experiences (ACEs), and researchers have examined the impact of people's "ACE score" on their lives, along with the resulting problems associated with having a high score. ACEs include experiences such as abuse (sexual, physical, emotional), neglect (physical and emotional), parental separation, witnessing violence, and parental substance abuse. After reading the discussion of family history in chapter 5, you should have a good idea about whether ACEs and accumulative little-t traumas are affecting your romantic life. In fact, one of the most common symptoms of this type of trauma is having impaired interpersonal relationships.

One significant element that determines what becomes traumatic for us involves how our brains process and store memories from traumatic events. There is some evidence that traumatic memories are stored in the part of the brain that is also responsible for emotions and sensations. Memories can also become repressed (pushed deep into the unconscious mind) or dissociated (blanked out) to cope with the stress associated with them. This contributes to your reactivity, or triggers, in the present, the cause of which you may not always be able to identify. Uncovering distressing memories and "reprocessing" (re-storing) them is often a substantial part of therapy. Storing them differently in your brain is essential, so that you are not reliving the effects over and over. Reprocessing them also allows you to better understand the emotions and bodily sensations associated with the memories.

Not all individuals exposed to adverse events and sudden

trauma develop post-traumatic stress disorder. Some do not even have any impaired functioning, for that matter. How trauma and adverse events affect you often depends upon several predisposing factors, such as your past experiences, perceptions of what happened to you, expectations, prior level of functioning, ability to tolerate stress, support system, resources, and so on. For these reasons, the development of trauma-reaction symptoms varies from person to person. Your ability to face and process the experience on your own or with others is also a factor in your ability to cope and move forward from it. Many people avoid triggering situations, numb out, or conceal their symptoms rather than deal with them head-on. This is not a sign of weakness but a common way to cope. It does not work effectively, though. Their inner voice tells these people that others are not safe or trustworthy, to never ask for help, and to just forge ahead. Getting professional help using trauma-informed treatment approaches is the only way to truly heal from big-T or little-t trauma if it is affecting you.

Avoidance is how Bree coped with her little-t trauma. She was emotionally neglected as a child. Her father was a functional alcoholic who had trouble keeping a job, so her mother had to work excessively to make ends meet. Bree was the "good daughter" who tried her best not to cause any more stress for her parents. She did well in school and became a successful lawyer. She was in a relationship with someone who worked all the time, and she told herself she was "fine" with that because she had no time to dedicate to her social life anyway. The problem was that she always felt mildly depressed and could not shake it. She chose not to ask for help, to avoid "burdening" anyone. She was so self-reliant and intelligent that she could not understand why she could not help herself eliminate her feelings of depression.

One day, a friend of Bree's, who happened to be a thera-pist, told her she might be experiencing the impact of trauma. Bree was incredulous at this suggestion, but after reading up on trauma online she realized her friend was indeed correct. Her work was a way to avoid dealing with the pain of her childhood experiences and other feelings. She'd never felt her life was in danger while growing up, but she hadn't felt she could just be a kid, have fun, and let her guard down. She'd had to be ultra-responsible and self-disciplined, and to basically parent herself in order to survive. She was finally ready to face the fact that this had taken a heavy toll on her and she needed to deal with it.

Bree wasn't weak for admitting she had a problem that re-quired professional help. Quite the opposite — she was strong and brave for acknowledging her problem and seeking help for it. Trauma is, in large part, considered a "disconnection problem." It does not improve in isolation — when the trau-matized person is disconnected from others. It is impossible to fully process your thoughts and feelings about what happened to you on your own. It requires the assistance of someone else, most often a therapist, to examine and integrate your under-standing of yourself, others, and the world in a new way.

Addiction

Another by-product of trauma and/or adverse early life expe-riences is addiction. Defining addiction is difficult, because it can mean different things to different people. Even profession-als have trouble reaching consensus on the definition and on what causes addiction. The overwhelming opinion is that ad-diction is characterized by someone's inability to consistently abstain from using a substance or from destructive behavior. There is a continuous craving and pursuit of the relief or re-ward from the substance or behavior, despite its leading to negative psychological, biological, relational, and spiritual consequences. The addicted person most often lacks insight into and recognition of the problems that arise from the behavior, including its impact on their emotional responses and interpersonal relationships. Denial can be a powerful and dangerous undercurrent that prevents the acknowledgment of addiction's impact. Addiction is frequently viewed as a disease of the brain and its circuitry. Akin to other chronic diseases and conditions, addiction usually has cycles of relapse and remission. Addiction requires active treatment recovery to overcome it.

Love Addiction

Can someone be addicted to love? Based on the above description, the answer is yes, a person can be addicted to love or to another person. If you are experiencing love addiction, you engage in repetitive unhealthy behaviors with another person that prompt you to compulsively seek a "reward" — attention, affection, love, sex, and so on. There are probably times you have broken up with that person (been in "remission), only to go back ("relapse") again. You find that the cravings for this person and ability to control yourself by staying away are insurmountable. If you think about the other relationships in your life, you may realize that these people are concerned about you and want to help you. They have tried to talk some sense into you, to persuade you to move on without Mr. Wrong, or to stop dating awful people in general, but you can't seem to do it. There is an unhealthy — perhaps even pathological — attachment to the love and sex that you experience with this person.

Here are some of the characteristics of love addiction:

- You seem unable to stop seeing a particular person despite knowing he is destructive or otherwise unhealthy for you.

- You get a reward, or "high," from the romance, pursuit, sex, or fantasy.
- You use relationships to cope with unhappiness or life stress.
- Your life generally seems chaotic.
- You fear being alone or find it unbearable to feel lonely.
- You confuse sex and sexual chemistry for love.
- You do whatever it takes not to lose your romantic partner, even if it goes against your values or who you feel you are inside.
- You repeatedly get into bad romantic relationships for extended periods of time.

Love addiction characteristics happen in a repetitive pattern, and possibly have done so throughout your adult life. Sex addiction, unlike love addiction, centers on the sexual act, risky sexual behavior, and other paraphilias, such as voyeurism, anonymous sex, excessive porn watching, and so on. Both types of addiction, however, will have you incessantly looking for someone or something outside yourself to give you what you think is lacking. With love addicts, it is often an intense and stimulating romantic experience, perhaps used to create the feeling of being valued, needed, or loved. All addictions, whether love, sex, or chemical, can be helped through concerted recovery efforts.

Psychotherapy for Trauma, Addiction, and Other Disorders

If you decide to get therapy for the relational distress you are experiencing, and if, after a thorough assessment, it is determined that traumatic and addictive processes are involved, your treatment plan will entail a multifaceted approach. Here is some of what you might work on with a skilled clinician:

- Learning to respond realistically to those you are in a relationship with, in a way that is appropriate
- Learning to accurately interpret the responses of those you are in a relationship with
- Maintaining emotional balance
- Accessing and identifying emotions, particularly those involving shame
- Coping in an optimistic and healthy way with relational stress
- Understanding the how and why of your reactions
- Experiencing your reactions in a safe and secure environment
- Embracing a healthy sense of selfishness that focuses you on self-care, boundaries, and your own personal needs
- Developing a view of yourself as someone who is not a victim, neither damaged nor helpless
- Making sense of your early history and FOO experiences
- Facing, instead of avoiding, any traumatic memories and the feelings, beliefs, and thoughts that come with them
- Experiencing the therapist as a "secure base" in order to develop an inner sense of safety and security
- Letting go of the need to control (and the illusion of control)
- Capitalizing on your strengths

Recovery

As briefly discussed in chapter 10, the dictionary definition of *recovery* is "a return to a normal state after a period of difficulty." *Recovering* is defined as "the act or process of returning to a normal state after a period of difficulty." These definitions are spot-on, succinct, and not at all demoralizing or stigmatizing. But I do wish to add one key point: the state you "return to" may not be a state of functioning or health that you previously experienced. The state may be different — a new normal. It may be a state in which you have integrated your past into your life in a way that helps you thrive today, and which will help you do so in the future. We recover from things *all the time*. Recovery is possible; it is not beyond your reach.

Recovering from trauma and/or addiction requires you to be able to emotionally process it, make sense of what happened to you, and develop healthy strategies to live your life differently. As previously stated, people often cannot effectively do this by themselves. You must allow a trustworthy person, often a therapist, in to help you share it, hold it, understand it, and let it go. Going to get help and making recovery your foremost priority will offer one of the best guarantees that you will break free from unending partner-choice struggles. But what exactly is involved in recovery, and how do you know you have officially recovered?

Recovery is another concept whose definition does not have a consensus. It is often used to describe sobriety, or abstinence from drinking or drug use. But this definition can also be complicated, since we know people may stop using addictive drugs or drink but continue to display problematic traits or behaviors. With respect to relationships, it's useful to generally define *recovery* as "voluntarily maintaining a lifestyle of interpersonally healthy relationships." There's a parallel between addiction to relationships and addiction to food, however: you still need food to live, since you can't abstain from eating and be healthy; you also can't (or shouldn't) abstain from relationships. If you still desire a romantic relationship, then aim to have one that does not cause you emotional pain.

Recovery requires you to use both your internal resources (for example, strengths, abilities) and external resources (for example, therapy, self-help books, groups) to be successful. There is a great deal of self-determination and personal choice when it comes to recovery. What you do to recover must be meaningful and valuable to you. It is also acceptable to know that you might mess up, make a mistake, and fall off track. This in no way means you aren't making progress or are not still "working" on your recovery. Making personal changes is almost never a perfectly straight path, anyway. There are always backslides and hiccups along the way. It may be comforting to know that the longer you work on your problems and stay focused on your goals, the easier it becomes and the easier it is to maintain progress.

A major point about recovery is that you can think of it as a tailored approach for you and your situation. It can involve several areas of focus that are important to you. For instance, your recovery efforts may include reading self-help books, going to individual and group therapy, attending religious or spiritual services, and keeping a journal. There are many pathways you can take to get better. The path you decide upon is self-directed and collaborative with others who are there to help you. You should surround yourself with people you consider allies in your efforts. And it is crucial to always maintain hope and show gratitude for small changes you make along the way — and for those things you do not need to change!

Success in recovery exists on a continuum of improved overall wellness and relationships. Only you can really decide whether you have achieved your goals and are functioning in a way that you are satisfied with. Here are some questions to ask yourself to determine if you are well on the road to successful recovery:

- Are you able to resist getting back into or staying in an unhealthy relationship?
- Have you prioritized what you have defined as part of your recovery efforts above all else?
- Do you believe you are taking good care of yourself and your needs?
- Are you continuously working toward your goals?
- Do you have one or more things (hobbies, interests, work) you feel passionate about?
- Are you coping well with negative emotions and stress?
- Do you have a good sense of what you can and can't control?
- Do you have a network of healthy and supportive friends?
- Are you able to relax and enjoy yourself?
- Do you generally feel fulfilled or as if you have a sense of purpose?

I explore some of these elements of recovery in the next chapter. I have included a general summary of recovery here, however, because it is something most often discussed in the context of mental health or addiction treatment and worked on with the guidance of a professional. Keeping the elements of recovery in mind will help you devise a treatment plan that keeps you on track to reach your goals during therapy. Be sure to remember to focus on progress, not perfection.

Liberating yourself from painful repetitive patterns in relationships is something you should not try to do on your own. There is a very good possibility that you have underestimated how detrimental such patterns have been to your psychological health. Do not let fear, pride, or stubbornness inhibit you from getting outside help. Commit to helping the most important person — you — not someone else. Take the initial step to make your life better by seeking help. In the next and final chapter, we will look at how to stay motivated, embrace self-love and self-forgiveness, and derive purpose and meaning from your relationship experiences.

CHAPTER THIRTEEN

THE MOST IMPORTANT PERSON: YOU

When you value yourself more than anything or any-one else, you can transform your life. Your world will spring wide open with hope and possibility. No one will be al-lowed to hold more power over you than you do. No one will define who you are or what you are worthy of. It is time you realize that the most important person in your life is YOU.

Leveraging Your Strengths

Most people must make an effort to think positively instead of negatively. As we have determined, being on constant alert for danger has, at least from an evolutionary standpoint, helped us survive as a species. An unintended consequence is that it also has pushed us to have a *negativity bias*. Several "waves" of psychology have occurred over time, bringing us new ways to understand and help people. One such wave, called *positive psychology*, that came through the field encouraged us to look at our strengths instead of our weaknesses, and at what is working instead of what is not working. The positive philosophy also emphasizes human strengths and the pursuit of happiness. A constant focus on dysfunction and disease is viewed as both undesirable and possibly even harmful. Maintaining such a pessimistic view takes away our perception that we have choices in how we think and behave.

Another benefit of modifying your thinking to a more positive style is that it helps "rewire" your brain. Something we know from neuroscience is that the brain has the ability to form and reorganize neural connections, a concept called *neuroplasticity*. The brain's neurons can "fire" in different patterns. When the brain changes these neural networks, the new patterns get stronger. This occurs commonly after we learn something new. We can adjust our thinking and focus on our strengths to help establish a more optimistic outlook. Doing so will affirm your mental toughness and make you a happier person.

The first step in leveraging your strengths is to take an inventory of them. Do not downplay or minimize any possible strength! It's time to boast a bit and bask in the glory of your positive attributes. Think about what comes to mind on your own, as well as feedback and compliments you have been given by others or direct feedback from school or work in the form of grades or raises.

Here are some questions to help you create a thorough list of strengths:

- What concrete skills or abilities have you acquired through work, education, or specialized training?

- What do you enjoy or feel passionate about because you are a natural or proficient at it?
- What positive feedback have you gotten from employers, teachers, family, or friends?
- Do you have any unique talents?
- What are your endearing inner qualities? (Examples: nonjudgmental, honest, kind, generous, loving, charismatic, spiritual, charitable, humorous, impartial, curious.)
- What are your appealing physical qualities? (Examples: physically fit, energetic, strong, attractive.)
- What have you accomplished that most people haven't or that is assumed to be difficult to achieve?

If you want to find a way to become energized, hopeful, and optimistic, spend time focusing on these strengths. Catch yourself when you are thinking pessimistically, and immediately think about the strengths you have listed here. You will unleash much more potential by doing so. You will also be cementing a new habit that activates a new neural pathway.

Self-Love

Loving yourself is a good idea. I'm talking not about the narcissistic version of self-love but about the version where you have positive regard for your own well-being and happiness. You absolutely should love yourself! I don't believe you have to love yourself *before* you can love someone else (as it is popular to say). But you can certainly do the best job of loving yourself. Women who pour themselves into relationships, especially bad ones, find that they neglect their own needs and contentment. They have not been loving or kind toward themselves, even if it is unintentional.

What does self-love look like, sound like, and feel like? Here are some examples:

- Putting yourself first, even if it upsets someone else
- Forgiving yourself for past mistakes or transgressions
- Candidly expressing yourself
- Responding to your body's need for rest, comfort, and nurturing
- Accepting yourself and the mix of positives, negatives, and imperfections
- Allowing yourself to feel deserving
- Embracing joy
- Knowing that you can change and grow
- Asking yourself, instead of others, for approval
- Not waiting for anyone else to create a life you love
- Protecting yourself from those who do you harm

Self-love is an ongoing practice, not an endpoint. It can influence your choices in love, work, and friendships. It can boost your ability to cope with distress. Behaving lovingly and kindly toward yourself will help you live with integrity and intention.

A Sense of Purpose

Let's talk a little more about a particular element of your recovery and personal growth efforts: having a sense of purpose. All humans need a sense of purpose; without it, we mentally suffer. Without purpose, you will meander pointlessly through life. It will make you susceptible to the undesirable behavior and moods discussed throughout this book. For example, your tendency to continuously try to fix your relationship with someone emotionally unavailable can be a way of trying to alleviate the pain you feel in response to it. It can become your purpose in a sense, an unhealthy one that will never leave you in peace. Alternatively, having a healthy and invigorating sense of purpose, and engaging in work and activities that bring joy and satisfaction, will help you thrive in life and your relationships.

Chelsea realized she had little or no sense of purpose during times when she wasn't with or obsessing over Tom. After it appeared they were broken up for good, she sought professional help. Her therapist guided her in her recovery efforts and in determining what might give her a sense of purpose to lift her mood and bring her fulfillment. She'd always loved animals, but Tom hated animals and often made it very difficult for her to take care of her dog, Riley. She felt incredibly guilty about having left Riley alone so much because of her relationship with Tom. Now that this tumultuous relationship was over, Chelsea decided to volunteer at the local animal shelter. She absolutely loved being there. She met several other kindhearted animal lovers and easily connected with them whenever she spent time at the shelter. Many of the dogs bonded with her, and it brought her such joy to help care for them. She also celebrated when "her dogs" got adopted. She always looked forward to volunteering at the shelter, and she was surprised at how great a sense of purpose it gave her.

Having purpose alleviates that sense of restlessness you get when your attention isn't occupied by external situations such as your romantic life. By focusing attention outward, you channel your mental energy into something useful and purposeful. It is not directed inward, on yourself, your negative mood, obsessive thoughts, and so on. It is valuable to think about being part of something bigger than yourself, especially when it involves helping humankind (or "animalkind," for that matter!). Doing so will improve your sense of achievement, self-worth, self-esteem, confidence, and well-being.

There are several core areas to focus on when figuring out your sense of purpose. You can expand on one that already exists — for example, getting more involved in your religion or exploring another one that you believe may appeal to you. Since the religious infrastructure is already in place, there are locations for people to congregate in order to practice the religion and socialize with others who have the same belief system.

Some people get their sense of purpose quite differently, through achievement. This achievement might be a level of success, wealth, or status. Other people, on the contrary, derive purpose from altruistic action: instead of thinking about their own circumstances, they think about those of others. They are driven to help others, improve society, contribute to righting injustice, better the environment, and so on. This brand of purpose may be particularly relevant to those who find themselves often trying unsuccessfully to help or better a partner. This is energy that can be diverted into something or some organization that would really benefit from their skills and efforts.

Many people derive a sense of purpose from intentional personal development. I encourage you to develop yourself educationally or creatively. Allowing yourself to let out your talents, make use of your ingenuity, and express yourself is invigorating. You may wish to try your hand at something new and develop an interest or skill set in an area you haven't yet explored. You might also consider exploring something less tangible that creates personal transformation, such as meditation practices, spiritual channeling, spiritual traditions such as Buddhism, or mystical practices like Kabbalah. There is a multitude of options for creating a purpose-driven life.

Letting Go of Control

You may not be tuned in to a big part of the dynamic between you and others that involves your "need" to control them. It is fundamental to recognize that this is often at play in many of the relationships you find yourself in. You must let go of any need, motivation, or desire to control or manage another person. You must learn where you "end" and another person "begins." You must admit that you can control only yourself. If what you are getting from a partner is not acceptable to you, stop trying to change *him*. You have two difficult choices: to accept him as is, or to move on.

In a relationship with someone emotionally unavailable — if you haven't cut your losses early — you might have a tendency to want to help, fix, protect, or rescue. As natural as it is to want to do this with someone we care about, someone we perceive as stuck or struggling, it works only in Hollywood movies. In real life, it makes things worse because it doesn't work — period. Furthermore, one truth you should embrace is that not everyone *wants* to change, and that's okay. Just as it is okay for you to make the decision about whether you want to change something about yourself, everyone else has the same prerogative.

Helping others is often the right thing to do. It can be confusing to figure out when it is okay to help and when you should pull back. In general, you should never consistently do something for someone that they can readily do for themselves. And you should never help someone who does not want it. In a romantic relationship, ask yourself if your partner has asked for help to be a better person or partner to you. Ask him if he wants to change. Ask him if it is important to him to make changes that will help him become more emotionally responsive to you. If the answer is not an unequivocal "yes," then it is time to back off.

This is exactly what Sophia tried. She was always attempting to help her boyfriend, Doug, by giving him advice and direction, especially on parenting. He was a guilt-ridden divorced dad who always seemed down on his luck. Sophia was a bright and bubbly schoolteacher. She watched as Doug disciplined the kids inconsistently, got easily manipulated by them, and spent money he didn't have on them to keep them happy. Sophia could clearly see he was creating little monsters, and it drove her berserk! She would buy him highly rated parenting books to read, which then sat gathering dust on the nightstand. She sent him articles and blogs online. She would sometimes directly advise him that he was "too emotional to be rational" with his kids. It began to cause fights and tension between them regularly.

One day, Sophia asked him point-blank, "Doug, do you honestly want my help or not when it comes to your kids?" He replied that he felt good about how he parented and that he was doing what he thought was right. So, no, he did not want Sophia's help. In fact, he said, he would prefer that she stop the constant critiquing and just leave the topic alone. She did what he asked, but it was nearly impossible. Soon it became unbearable for her to just sit idly by. She started to feel anxious and hopeless. She realized she was never going to have control over this circumstance. She could not even positively influence Doug in the area of parenting. She decided to take a break from the relationship to think about her future and whether being a stepmother one day was right for her. In the process, she realized the problem was no longer about Doug and his parenting skills. It was her pattern of getting into relationships with people who needed fixing. She decided she was not going to rescue, help, or overfunction anymore. She was determined to change herself, not someone else.

When you stop trying to control someone else, you empower yourself in ways you may not have expected. You can shift that energy onto something that *is* changeable. In some situations, you may begin to recognize aspects of *yourself* that you wish to change instead. You will no longer be deflecting outward but looking inward. When you stop controlling others, you will likely start focusing on what the actual problem is (and it won't be what you thought it was) and find that you can effectively solve it.

Facing Loss

When you think about loss, you probably think about the death of someone you care about, someone close to you. However, we experience many small and big losses (and everything in between) throughout our lives. Indeed, death is a significant loss; but in the context of loss, don't discount the impact of a relationship ending or a dream not being realized. In chapter 9, I discussed the feelings that go along with loss and how to cope with them and get through that loss. With loss, there is an element of personal growth. Experiencing loss is an absolute in life. How well you adapt and adjust afterward is instrumental in your growth as an individual. The point is that loss is *normal*. There is no way to prevent the natural flow of life, and life includes loss and unanticipated changes. Allowing yourself to embrace this truth will free you, but you will also be giving yourself a tremendous gift, one that you deserve!

Forgiveness

Making the decision to forgive someone who hurt you is an extremely personal choice. It may come as a result of your core values, religious or spiritual beliefs, your opinions, the opinions of others, or what you have been taught throughout your life. You may firmly believe that some wrongdoings in life are just not forgivable. This is okay. Forgiveness is often less about the person who transgressed and more about how forgiveness can help you heal. Some people believe — and it makes sense — that you should not forgive people who aren't repentant for what they did to you. In relationship situations, when someone treats you poorly, often that person offers little or no recognition of what he did to you — or there is finger-pointing that goes around in a vicious circle. In such cases you are not likely to get the heartfelt apology you deserve.

When contemplating whether to forgive or not forgive, base your decision on whether it will help *you*. Forgiving does not mean you condone or excuse the behavior. It does not mean you need to let the person know you forgive him or her. And it doesn't mean you are going to forget what happened and will not have feelings about it. It means you have found your own personal way in which to accept the reality of what happened, to let go, manage its impact on your life, and move forward. Forgiving is entirely up to you, and you should do it if it feels right and will be helpful to you.

The flip side of forgiving someone else is forgiving *your-self*. Sometimes it is more difficult to forgive yourself than to forgive others. We seem to want to hang on to things and beat ourselves up. We also hate to admit how wrong or stupid we were. It just feels awful! Newsflash: You are human! No one is perfect. No one gets it right all the time. As you can imagine, not forgiving yourself will also not help you move forward. You may not realize how freeing and invigorating it is to for-give yourself for what you think were bad behaviors or bad choices that you made along the way with men. Realize that you did the best you could do at the time, based on what you knew. Think about the lesson it taught you, what it helped you realize about yourself, and how it helped you define your values. This is the part you can take away and keep; the rest you need to throw away.

Being Vulnerable

In your quest for love, you will experience a sense of exposure and susceptibility to emotional harm. Finding love supervenes risk-taking, courage, and emotional exposure. It involves uncertainty and ambiguity during the process. This is one of the harshest truths to accept. There's no escape from this reality; the only path to love is to lean into it and march straight through.

Finding the way to being brave and feeling worthy of safe and secure love doesn't happen spontaneously for anyone. It is nourished daily through intentional choices that move you in the direction of the goals you have laid out. Being vulnerable is at the core of the choices you make and the practices you engage in. It's about how you respond in the face of inevitable ambiguity. Vulnerability is what makes the resulting experiences meaningful and purposeful.

One of the underpinnings of what makes us feel vulnerable in romantic relationships is the idea that we are not good enough or worthy enough. It is critical that you banish this idea from your mind and repeat to yourself daily that you are enough and that you are worthy. You must always be looking for the proof, however small, that this is true. We tend to do the opposite, and it's not the least bit helpful to our human spirits and souls.

You are in no way required to be vulnerable to anyone who has not *earned the right* to receive it. It happens slowly and gradually as the building blocks get stacked in a mutual relationship (with anyone — romantic or platonic). As your sense of safety and your trust grow, vulnerability will follow.

Finding Meaning in Struggles

If your search for a meaningful romantic connection has been rife with struggles, you can benefit from finding the meaning and lessons that lie within those struggles. View pain as a hidden invitation to growth. You are stronger than you think you are to have come this far already. Now start exploring the significance of the pain.

Here are some questions to help you explore the meaning in your struggle:

- What did this experience teach me about myself, my life, or changes I need to make?
- Is there anything positive that came out of my experience?
- What did this experience teach me about my reaction to adversity?
- Have any opportunities emerged from this experience?
- Has this experience made me stronger?
- Has this experience exposed a weakness I need to work on?
- Did this experience help me bond with others who have been there too?
- Has this experience shifted my perspective on life (or something else) for the better?

No one is exempt from painful, even tragic, life events. Some of the biggest changes, or revelations about how you are living your life, can emerge from these trying times. You do not have to be thankful for or feel beholden to the experience itself, but you might perhaps be grateful for the meaning found in it and the lessons learned from it. It is your choice whether you will let the experience cripple or strengthen you.

Some Final Thoughts

Finding love — a peaceful, secure love — is one of the most awesome and rewarding experiences you can have during your lifetime. However, many of us do not understand how to find it or, worse, find ourselves in repetitive, painful patterns in our search for love. When we find ourselves in such a place, we try our best to make it better, make changes, or do things differently. Yet we often don't know how or even why we keep finding ourselves in these spots again and again. We wander aimlessly in our search for solutions.

Not every individual necessarily has the same capability or desire for love and intimacy that others have. Our hopes and fantasies about love may keep us believing that the search is the same for all of us. When your need for love, intimacy, closeness, and connection is met with fear, distance, withdrawal, and disconnection, trouble will brew. Finding someone with views about love that are similar to yours (and who has similar behaviors in response to love) will create the best possibility for love to flourish.

Finding love is a fallible endeavor. Love itself is far from perfect, and it is not the cure for all your troubles. Even if you have found "the one," you will have some ups and downs, some bumps in the road to navigate. This is why you want to choose your partner carefully. You want someone who won't bail or fall apart when the bumps are hit, especially if you have chosen to commit to this person.

Love requires vulnerability, risk-taking, and a tolerance for uncertainty. The person you have chosen to love (and who has chosen you) is the person you must reach for in times of emotional need. You must know what your needs are and how to ask for them to be met. If you are getting signals early on that your needs are insignificant, this not acceptable. Your needs are legitimate. Your desire to count on another person is valid. Someone who has historically demonstrated that he does not respond to your reaches is not going to be a life partner. If you are always meeting his needs and it is not mutual, you should not accept this as normal or okay.

I am confident you have found the many answers you are looking for if you have been struggling with romantic interests who are emotionally unavailable. I believe you now know what love should look and feel like. I expect you to not settle for someone who does not love and respond to you in the way to which you are entitled. I want you to realize you have choices and the power to think and act in ways that attract a loving, kind, and responsive partner. I hope you will use the information infused throughout this book to help you on your way to genuinely experiencing, finding, and keeping love that is mutual, dependable, and gratifying.

ACKNOWLEDGMENTS

First and foremost, I thank my husband, Michael, who has proved that an emotional and loving connection can thrive when one chooses the right life partner. I am forever grateful for my two daughters, Jamie and Mandy, who, along with my husband, have been my cheerleaders throughout this book-writing journey. Also, my friends and family, too many to list, have been deeply supportive and have shown genuine interest in my writing. I am profoundly grateful to have all these people in my life.

The idea for the premise of this book arose during my media psychology course in my doctoral program. My book proposal was written under the guidance of Dr. Jonathan Rich, who predicted early on that I might really have something here! I am thankful for his positive words and for his taking the time to review my proposal and provide feedback. He also directed me to the invaluable resources necessary for transforming the proposal into a real live book.

I am especially thankful for my agent, MaryAnn Karinch, of the Rudy Agency, for her expertise and for taking a chance on representing me and my book. She believed in this project and worked hard to find a publisher so that this book would become a reality.

I also thank the staff at New World Library and my editor,

Georgia Hughes, for taking a chance on a first-time author. Her wisdom, guidance, expert feedback, and insights have been invaluable to me in the writing of this book. I am incredibly appreciative of copyeditor Bonita Hurd's thorough and insightful edits and suggestions as well.

As this book evolved from idea to proposal to full-length manuscript, there were several draft editors along the way. I thank Hannah Eason, Ralph Hickok, Hilary Gunning, and Liz Seif, for helping refine the material. I am also thankful for the help of my colleague Cina Hoey, LCSW, for offering to be a beta reader and providing valuable feedback.

My freelance writing (and now authoring) would not have been possible without some of the platforms that provided national exposure. In this regard, I especially thank Melanie Gorman, senior vice president, along with the staff, of Your-Tango media for expert coaching and guidance.

I learned to do my work as a clinician over the course of many, many years, through much reading and formal education. However, it has also been inspired, molded, and refined by two gifted clinicians: Michael Barnett, LPC, and Dr. Jennifer Leigh. Thank you for mentoring and guiding me to become a better clinician myself over the past few years. I also thank my colleague and friend Jessica Marchena, LMHC, for other work-project collaboration and stimulating conversation on emotionally focused couples' therapy and beyond.

Finally, I am indebted to the numerous clients who have trusted me to help them heal their pain and find serenity and love. Their sharing provided a way for the psychological concepts in this book to come to life to help countless other people. It has been an honor to be their therapist and, many times, their "secure attachment figure."

RECOMMENDED RESOURCES

The following are recommended resources on some topics discussed in this book that you may wish to gain further knowledge about. This list is by no means exhaustive.

Books

Addiction and Codependency

Beattie, Melody. *Codependent No More: How to Stop Controlling Others and Start Caring for Yourself.* Center City, MN: Hazelden, 1992.

Mellody, Pia, Andrea Wells Miller, and Keith Miller. *Facing Love Addiction: Giving Yourself the Power to Change the Way You Love.* San Francisco: Harper, 2003.

Norwood, Robin. *Women Who Love Too Much: When You Keep Wishing and Hoping He'll Change.* New York: Simon & Schuster, 1986.

Attachment

Karen, Robert. *Becoming Attached: First Relationships and How They Shape Our Capacity to Love.* New York: Oxford University Press, 1994.

Lovenheim, Peter. *The Attachment Effect: Exploring the Powerful Ways Our Earliest Bond Shapes Our Relationships and Lives.* New York: TarcherPerigee, 2018.

Dating

Levine, Amir, and Rachel Heller. *Attached: The New Science of Adult Attachment and How It Can Help You Find and Keep Love.* New York: Penguin, 2012.

Tatkin, Stan. *Wired for Dating: How Understanding Neurobiology and Attachment Style Can Help You Find Your Ideal Mate.* Oakland, CA: New Harbinger, 2016.

Emotion

Barrett, Lisa Feldman. *How Emotions Are Made: The Secret Life of the Brain.* New York: Houghton Mifflin Harcourt, 2017.

Goleman, Daniel. *Emotional Intelligence: Why It Can Matter More Than IQ.* New York: Bantam, 2006.

Family Dysfunction

Black, Claudia. *It Will Never Happen to Me: Growing Up with Addiction as Youngsters, Adolescents, Adults.* Center City, MN: Hazelden, 2002.

Forward, Susan, and Craig Buck. *Toxic Parents: Overcoming Their Hurtful Legacy and Reclaiming Your Life.* New York: Bantam, 2001.

Love

Fisher, Helen. *Why We Love: The Nature and Chemistry of Romantic Love.* New York: Henry Holt, 2004.

Johnson, Sue. *Love Sense: The Revolutionary New Science of Romantic Relationships.* New York: Little, Brown, 2013.

Relationships

Johnson, Sue. *Hold Me Tight: Seven Conversations for a Lifetime of Love.* New York: Little, Brown, 2008.

Tatkin, Stan. *Wired for Love: How Understanding Your Partner's Brain and Attachment Style Can Help You Defuse Conflict and Build a Secure Relationship.* Oakland, CA: New Harbinger, 2012.

Vulnerability

Brown, Brené. *Daring Greatly: How the Courage to Be Vulnerable Transforms the Way We Live, Love, Parent, and Lead.* New York: Penguin, 2015.

Workbooks

Hay, Louise. *Love Yourself, Heal Your Life Workbook.* Insight Guide. Carlsbad, CA: Hay House, 1990.

Hayes, Steven. *Get out of Your Mind & into Your Life: The New Acceptance & Commitment Therapy.* Oakland, CA: New Harbinger, 2005.

McKay, Matthew, Patrick Fanning, and Patricia Zurita Ona. *Mind and Emotions: A Universal Treatment for Emotional Disorders.* Oakland, CA: New Harbinger, 2011.

McKay, Matthew, Jeffrey Wood, and Jeffrey Brantley. *The Dialectical Behavior Therapy Skills Workbook: Practical DBT Exercises for Learning Mindfulness, Interpersonal Effectiveness, Emotion Regulation and Distress Tolerance.* Oakland, CA: New Harbinger, 2010.

Schirladi, Glenn. *The Self-Esteem Workbook.* Oakland, CA: New Harbinger, 2016.

Stahl, Bob, and Elisha Goldstein. *A Mindfulness-Based Stress Reduction Workbook.* Oakland, CA: New Harbinger, 2010.

REFERENCES

"24 Ways to Put Your Strengths to Work." *VIA Blog*, January 21, 2016. www.viacharacter.org/blog/24-ways-to-put-your-strengths-to-work/.

"Adverse Childhood Experiences." Substance Abuse and Mental Health Services Administration. Updated September 5, 2017. www.samhsa. gov/capt/practicing-effective-prevention/prevention-behavioral -health/adverse-childhood-experiences.

Ainsworth, Mary, M. C. Blehar, E. Walters, and S. Wall. *Patterns of Attachment: A Psychological Study of the Strange Situation*. Hillsdale, NJ: Lawrence Erlbaum Associates, 1978.

Back, Mitja D., Stefan C. Schmukle, and Boris Egloff. "Why Are Narcissists So Charming at First Sight? Decoding the Narcissism-Popularity Link at Zero Acquaintance." *Journal of Personality and Social Psychology* 98, no. 1 (2010): 132. https://doi.org/10.1037/a0016338.

Badenoch, Bonnie. *Being a Brain-Wise Therapist: A Practical Guide to Interpersonal Neurobiology*. Norton Series on Interpersonal Neurobiology. New York: W. W. Norton, 2008.

Barbash, Elyssa. "Different Types of Trauma: Small 't' versus Large 'T.'" *Psychology Today* (blog), March 13, 2017. www.psychologytoday.com /us/blog/trauma-and-hope/201703/different-types-trauma-small-t -versus-large-t.

Baumeister, Roy F., Karen Dale, and Kristin L. Sommer. "Freudian Defense Mechanisms and Empirical Findings in Modern Social Psychology: Reaction Formation, Projection, Displacement, Undoing, Isolation, Sublimation, and Denial." *Journal of Personality* 66, no. 6 (1998): 1081–1124. https://doi.org/10.1111/1467-6494.00043.

Bowlby, John. *Attachment and Loss*. New York: Basic Books, 1969.

Brown, Brené. *Daring Greatly: How the Courage to Be Vulnerable Transforms the Way We Live, Love, Parent, and Lead.* New York: Penguin, 2015.

Brubacher, Lorrie. "Emotionally Focused Individual Therapy: An Attachment-Based Experiential/Systemic Perspective." *Person-Centered & Experiential Psychotherapies* 16, no. 1 (2017): 50–67. http://dx.doi.org /10.1080/14779757.2017.1297250.

———. *Stepping into Emotionally Focused Couple Therapy: Key Ingredients of Change.* London: Karnac Books, 2018.

Cheskeski, Laura. "Take the ACE Quiz — and Learn What It Does and Doesn't Mean." *NPR.* March 2, 2015. www.npr.org/sections/health-shots/2015/03/02/387007941/take-the-ace-quiz-and-learn-what-it -does-and-doesnt-mean/.

Clark, Josh. "What Are Emotions and Why Do We Have Them?" *How Stuff Works*, September 13, 2010. https://science.howstuffworks.com/ life/what-are-emotions.htm/.

Collins, Bryn. *Emotional Unavailability: Recognizing It, Understanding It, and Avoiding Its Trap.* New York: McGraw-Hill Professional, 1998.

"The Complete Guide to Goal-Setting." *Life Coach Spotter*, n.d. www .lifecoachspotter.com/goal-setting/.

Courtois, Christine A., and Julian D. Ford. *Treatment of Complex Trauma: A Sequenced, Relationship-Based Approach.* New York: Guilford, 2012.

DePompo, Paul, and Misa Butsuhara. "The 'Other' Side of Infidelity: The Experience of the 'Other' Partner, Anxious Love, and Implications for Practitioners." *Psychological Thought* 9, no. 1 (2016): 41–57. https://psyct.psychopen.eu/article/view/167/html.

———. *The Other Woman's Affair: Gambling Your Heart and Reclaiming Your Life When Your Partner Is Married.* Newport Beach, CA: CBTI of Southern California, 2016.

Diamond, Stephen A. "Essential Secrets of Psychotherapy: Repetitive Relationship Patterns." *Psychology Today* (blog), January 14, 2008. www.psychologytoday.com/us/blog/evil-deeds/200806/essential -secrets-psychotherapy-repetitive-relationship-patterns/.

Feuerman, Marni. "A 5-Step Plan to Stop Being the Mistress and Finally Walk Away from an Affair." *Your Tango* (blog), February 9, 2018.

www.yourtango.com/experts/marni-feuerman/how-fall-out-love
-married-man.

———. "4 Brutal Truths about Why You Fall for Guys Who Don't Love You
Back." *Your Tango* (blog), March 31, 2016. www.yourtango.com/experts
/marni-feuerman/reasons-you-are-drawn-someone-who-wont-love
-you-back/.

———. "The Science of Love 101." *Your Tango* (blog), November 8, 2014/.
www.yourtango.com/experts/marni-feuerman/science-love-101/.

———. "21 Signs You're in an Emotionally Abusive Relationship." *Your
Tango* (blog), January 25, 2016. www.yourtango.com/experts/marni
-feuerman/signs-abusive-relationship/.

———. "What Is Insecure Attachment Style?" *Verywell Mind*. Updated
January 25, 2018. www.verywellmind.com/marriage-insecure
-attachment-style-2303303/.

———. "Your Attachment Style Influences the Success of Your Relationship." *Gottman Relationship Blog*. Gottman Institute. February 24,
2017. www.gottman.com/blog/attachment-style-influences-success
-relationship/.

Fishbane, Mona DeKoven. *Loving with the Brain in Mind: Neurobiology
and Couple Therapy*. Norton Series on Interpersonal Neurobiology.
New York: W. W. Norton, 2013.

Fisher, Helen. *Why We Love: The Nature and Chemistry of Romantic
Love*. New York: Henry Holt, 2004.

Fitzgerald, MacLean. "Fear Conditioning: How Your Brain Learns about
Danger." Brain Connection. August 26, 2005. https://brainconnection
.brainhq.com/2005/08/26/fear-conditioning-how-the-brain-learns
-about-danger/.

Freedman, Gili, Darcey N. Powell, Benjamin Le, and Kipling D. Williams.
"Ghosting and Destiny: Implicit Theories of Relationships Predict
Beliefs about Ghosting." *Journal of Social and Personal Relationships*
(January 12, 2018). https://doi.org/10.1177/0265407517748791.

Goldsmith, Barton. "Understanding Emotion Is Important to Your Relationship." *Psychology Today* (blog), April 5, 2016. www.psychology
today.com/us/blog/emotional-fitness/201604/understanding
-emotions-is-important-your-relationship/.

Gottman, John. "The 3 Phases of Love." *Gottman Relationship Blog*.

Gottman Institute. November 19, 2014. www.gottman.com/blog/the -3-phases-of-love/.

Gottman, John, and Nan Silver. *The Seven Principles for Making Marriage Work: A Practical Guide from the Country's Foremost Relationship Expert.* New York: Harmony Books, 2015.

"Group Therapy." *GoodTherapy.* Updated February 5, 2018. www .goodtherapy.org/learn-about-therapy/modes/group-therapy/.

Johnson, Sue. *Hold Me Tight: Seven Conversations for a Lifetime of Love.* New York: Little, Brown, 2008.

———. *Love Sense: The Revolutionary New Science of Romantic Relationships.* New York: Little, Brown, 2013.

Johnson, Susan M. *The Practice of Emotionally Focused Couple Therapy: Creating Connection.* New York: Routledge, 2012.

Karen, Robert. *Becoming Attached: First Relationships and How They Shape Our Capacity to Love.* New York: Oxford University Press, 1994.

Langeslag, Sandra, and Michelle Sanchez. "Down-Regulation of Love Feelings after a Romantic Break-Up: Self-Report and Electrophysiological Data." *Journal of Experimental Psychology* 147, no. 5 (2017): 720–733. www.ncbi.nlm.nih.gov/pubmed/28857575.

Levine, Amir, and Rachel Heller. *Attached: The New Science of Adult Attachment and How It Can Help You Find — and Keep — Love.* New York: Penguin, 2012.

Lipton, B., and D. Fosha. "Attachment as a Transformative Process in AEDP: Operationalizing the Intersection of Attachment Theory and Affective Neuroscience." *Journal of Psychotherapy Integration* 21, no. 3 (2011): 253. http://psycnet.apa.org/doi/10.1037/a0025421.

Lovenheim, Peter. *The Attachment Effect: Exploring the Powerful Ways Our Earliest Bond Shapes Our Relationships and Lives.* New York: TarcherPerigee, 2018.

Martin, Sharon. "Stop Trying to Change People Who Don't Want to Change." *Happily Imperfect* (blog). Updated April 22, 2018. https://blogs.psychcentral.com/imperfect/2018/04/stop-trying-to -change-people-who-dont-want-to-change/.

McKay, Matthew, Jeffrey Wood, and Jeffrey Brantley. *The Dialectical Behavior Therapy Skills Workbook: Practical DBT Exercises for*

Learning Mindfulness, Interpersonal Effectiveness, Emotion Regulation and Distress Tolerance. Oakland, CA: New Harbinger, 2010.

McLeod, Saul. "Cognitive Behavioral Therapy." SimplyPsychology. Updated 2015. www.simplypsychology.org/cognitive-therapy.html/.

Mikulincer, Mario, and Phillip R. Shaver. *Attachment in Adulthood: Structure, Dynamics, and Change.* New York: Guilford, 2007.

Minuchin, Salvador. *Families and Family Therapy.* Cambridge, MA: Harvard University Press, 1974.

Mizrahi, Moran, Gilad Hirschberger, Mario Mikulincer, Ohad Szepsenwol, and Gurit E. Birnbaum. "Reassuring Sex: Can Sexual Desire and Intimacy Reduce Relationship-Specific Attachment Insecurities?" *European Journal of Social Psychology* 46, no. 4 (2016): 467–480. http://dx.doi.org/10.1002/ejsp.2184.

Muller, Robert. "Love's End: Attachment and the Dissolution of a Relationship." *Psychology Today* (blog), February 7, 2014. www.psychology today.com/us/blog/talking-about-trauma/201402/loves-end -attachment-and-the-dissolution-relationship/.

Ni, Preston. "How to Spot and Stop Manipulators." *Psychology Today* (blog), June 1, 2014. www.psychologytoday.com/us/blog/communication -success/201406/how-spot-and-stop-manipulators/.

Nichols, Michael P., and Richard C. Schwartz. *The Essentials of Family Therapy.* Boston: Allyn and Bacon, 2014.

Norwood, Robin. *Women Who Love Too Much: When You Keep Wishing and Hoping He'll Change.* New York: Simon & Schuster, 1986.

Phillips, Lisa A. *Unrequited: The Thinking Woman's Guide to Romantic Obsession.* New York: HarperCollins, 2015.

Porges, Stephen. *The Polyvagal Theory: Neurophysiological Foundations of Emotions, Attachment, Communication, and Self-Regulation.* New York: Norton, 2011.

Porterfield, Traci. "9 Do's and Don'ts of Mindful Dating." Chopra Center. Accessed May 9, 2018. https://chopra.com/articles/9-dos-and-donts -of-mindful-dating/.

Reeve, Johnmarshall. *Understanding Motivation and Emotion.* Hoboken, NJ: John Wiley & Sons, 2015.

Roberts, Laura Morgan, Gretchen Spreitzer, Jane E. Dutton, Robert E. Quinn, Emily Heaphy, and Brianna Barker. "How to Play to Your

Strengths." *Harvard Business Review*, January 2005. https://hbr
.org/2005/01/how-to-play-to-your-strengths/.

Robinson, Lawrence, Melinda Smith, and Jeanne Segal. "Emotional and
Psychological Trauma." *HelpGuide*. Updated January 2018. www
.helpguide.org/articles/ptsd-trauma/coping-with-emotional
-and-psychological-trauma.htm/.

Schwarz, Robert. *Tools for Transforming Trauma*. New York: Routledge,
2013.

Seligman, Martin E. P. *Learned Optimism: How to Change Your Mind and
Your Life*. New York: Vintage, 2006.

Stolorow, Robert D. "A Non-pathologizing Approach to Emotional Trauma."
Psychology Today (blog), December 19, 2014. www.psychology
today.com/us/blog/feeling-relating-existing/201412/non
-pathologizing-approach-emotional-trauma/.

Subotnik, Rona B. *Will He Really Leave Her for Me?: Understanding Your
Situation, Making Decisions for Your Happiness*. New York: Simon &
Schuster, 2005.

Tatkin, Stan. *Wired for Dating: How Understanding Neurobiology and
Attachment Style Can Help You Find Your Ideal Mate*. Oakland, CA:
New Harbinger, 2016.

———. *Wired for Love: How Understanding Your Partner's Brain and
Attachment Style Can Help You Defuse Conflict and Build a Secure
Relationship*. Oakland, CA: New Harbinger, 2012.

Taylor, Steve. "The Power of Purpose." *Psychology Today* (blog), July 21,
2013. www.psychologytoday.com/us/blog/out-the-darkness/201307
/the-power-purpose/.

University of Cincinnati Learning Assistance Center. "Setting Goals for
Yourself, and Motivating Yourself to Succeed." University of Cincinnati. https://ferris.edu/HTMLS/colleges/university/eccc/pdf/setting
goals.pdf/.

Wallach, Suzanne M. "Insecure Attachment Style and Romantic Partner
Selection in Women with Emotionally Unavailable Fathers." PhD diss.,
Chicago School of Professional Psychology, 2014. https://search
.proquest.com/openview/c1760a05536850dd3ee7d63dced6b093/.

Walter, Ili. "Family of Origin Exploration for the Therapist: Family Rules
and Structure." *Family Therapy Basics* (blog), January 31, 2017.

http://familytherapybasics.com/blog/2017/1/31/family-of-origin
-exploration-for-the-therapist-family-rules-and-structure/.

——. "Family of Origin Exploration for the Therapist: 3 Steps for How
to Begin." *Family Therapy Basics* (blog), November 1, 2016.
http://familytherapybasics.com/blog/2016/10/31/family-of-origin
-exploration-for-the-therapist-3-steps-för-how-to-begin/.

Wakin, Albert, and Duyen B. Vo. "Love-Variant: The Wakin–Vo IDR Model
of Limerence." 2008. http://citeseerx.ist.psu.edu/viewdoc/download
?doi=10.1.1.729.1932&rep=rep1&type=pdf.

Whitbourne, Susan Krauss. "The Lure of the Unpredictable Lover." *Psychology Today* (blog), November 13, 2012. www.psychologytoday.com
/us/blog/fulfillment-any-age/201211/the-lure-the-unpredictable
-lover.

INDEX

221

ABOUT THE AUTHOR

Dr. Marni Feuerman is a licensed clinical social worker and a licensed marriage and family therapist. She holds a master's degree in social work and a doctorate in psychology. She maintains a private practice in the South Florida area, where she lives with her husband and twin daughters. The focus of her clinical work includes relationship problems, marriage, infidelity, dating, and divorce. She has specialized training in evidence-based couples' therapy and conducts workshops as well as therapy intensives. As a nationally recognized relationship and marriage expert, she has made contributions to and written articles for countless online media outlets. Dr. Feuerman is passionate about helping her clients work through their relationship struggles to find love and emotional connection. For more about this book and the author, visit www.drmarnionline.com.